Terran often resides at no fixed address in the Caribbean aboard a sailboat. Terran spends his free time tracking and writing about cutting-edge technologies.

His first book, titled *Money and Success is Mind Over Matter*, was published in 2015 as a tool for success for his sons. Terran carries forward the subject of success in this exciting new book, *New Secrets for Success in an AI World.*

Terran James

NEW SECRETS FOR SUCCESS IN AN AI WORLD

AUSTIN MACAULEY PUBLISHERS®

LONDON * CAMBRIDGE * NEW YORK * SHARJAH

Ordering Information
Quantity sales: Special discounts are available on quantity purchases by corporations, associations, and others. For details, contact the publisher at the address below.

Publisher's Cataloging-in-Publication data
James, Terran
New Secrets for Success in an AI World

ISBN 9781685623777 (Paperback)
ISBN 9781685624446 (ePub e-book)

Library of Congress Control Number: 2024916155

www.austinmacauley.com/us

First Published 2024
Austin Macauley Publishers LLC
40 Wall Street, 33rd Floor, Suite 3302
New York, NY 10005
USA

mail-usa@austinmacauley.com
+1 (646) 5125767

Table of Content

Doctor Andrew NG, one of the founding fathers of AI, says, 'AI is the new electricity. When electricity was first discovered, we didn't understand its potential to change the world.'

AI is already here and evolving much more quickly than you think!

Five things **you may not know about the current state of AI as of the end of 2023:**

1. Artificial intelligence is more common than many people think: 77% of people on the planet use AI, even though only 33% of people believe they do. Chatbots make up a significant percentage of this AI, as many companies use them to handle customer service inquiries, and the use of chatbots is only expected to increase.
2. The number of people already working on AI. There may be as few as 22,000 highly-trained AI specialists and up to 300,000 AI researchers and practitioners within broader technical teams.
3. The global artificial intelligence (AI) market size was estimated at USD 136.6 billion in 2022 and is expected to reach USD 196.6 billion in 2023.
4. The United States is the leader with 150 supercomputers among the world's 500 most powerful supercomputers. It is followed by China, with 134 supercomputers, and Germany, with 36 supercomputers.
5. 2023 was a surprising year for artificial intelligence with almost 7,000 tools (new applications).

- GPT-3 (OpenAI) The first in our list is GPT-3, short for Generative Pre-trained Transformer 3 is the third series of generative language models developed by OpenAI.
- AlphaGo (Google DeepMind).
- Watson (IBM).
- Sophia (Hanson Robotics).
- Tesla Autopilot (Tesla Inc.).

The true potential of AI lies in its ability to uplift humanity, while safeguarding and empowering future generations.

His Holiness Sri Amit Ray

- GPT-3 (OpenAI) The first in our list is GPT-3, short for Generative Pre-trained Transformer 3 is the third series of generative language models developed by OpenAI.

Author's Note

It's easy to dive off into the weeds and use technical jargon on a complex topic such as this.

Let me assure you this book was written for everyone. My intent is to make this book valuable and exciting. We live in a fascinating time; centenarians have seen massive technological changes over the last hundred years. It is astounding to think that the first commercially viable electronic computer was sold in Japan in 1950. Here we are 73 years later, facing the most significant technological ramp in the known history of human civilization. I am humbled and marvel at the exponential changes that are coming!

I personally believe that AI is a welcome breath of fresh air into a world society where money, greed, and power are far too prevalent. We need the tools as a society to transgress these natural human tendencies.

Not everyone shares this view; however, without AI on the horizon and careful management of our world, we may be ultimately pointed down a dark road. I sincerely believe humans will embrace new technologies positively and mostly non-destructively.

Some bad apples seem to be hell-bent on forcefully taking whatever they desire. Fortunately, when you look at the course of history, dictatorships are slowly becoming a thing of the past. Technology educates the masses, and all the new generations with global knowledge want freedom from oppression.

AI will bring us a new understanding of everything for everyone. It's easy to be pessimistic and focus on the negativity generated globally. Everyone must remember that communication now happens in the blink of an eye, often causing a knee-jerk reaction with global stock markets or the world is falling apart. Nothing could be further from the truth!

Once AI has modified our monetary system to a global currency that is fair and shared with everyone, we will have turned the corner into a new world of peace and prosperity. It's easy to blame politicians and large corporations for inadequacies in society or on a personal level. Culturing personal responsibility for action and accountability are the first steps to personal freedom. If you don't believe that things are improving over the long term for everyone on the planet, consider reviewing this poverty chart on Wikipedia, shown below.

Max Roser based on World Bank and Bourguignon and Morrisson (2002). https://ourworldindata.org/extreme-poverty

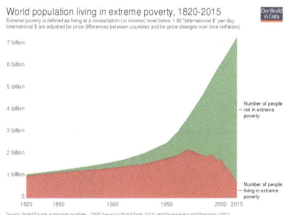

World population living in extreme poverty, 1820-2015

Foreword

Computers have already firmly placed us in the transforming technological age. AI is an accelerant that will open doors beyond what we ever dreamed possible! A glimpse into the future might include AI in your car to take you exactly where you want to go in an ultra-safe manner. AI will be in your home, taking the smart home concept to an entirely different level: think intelligent awareness. Your home will also know who you are, your family, and your friends. AI will communicate with you effectively wherever you are. Imagine an omnipresent intelligence monitoring the security and safety of your home and business.

AI-generated companions are already under development and can and will be your health advisor if needed. AI could monitor your vital signs and recommend dietary changes, exercise, and personal development recommendations. On other fronts, AI has already transformed weather prediction models such as hurricane tracking. This is creating an early warning system, making people safer. AI will eventually be in everything, communicating with you through your telephone, vehicle, and home and assisting you at work. In the bigger picture, technological changes are coming at an unprecedented rate. Advancements in healthcare, communications, travel, space exploration, human augmentation, energy, climate management, and solutions, to name a few.

You may be mistaken if you think this is way out on the horizon in some distant future timeline.

The short-term timeline for AI is a matter of months, and the medium timeline for developing some projects is three years. Longer-term development is often referred to as in this decade.

Code development creating new applications for AI is getting shorter all the time because as one application creates a baseline, it can then be used across many different applications. Recently, AI started writing code for new applications with growing complexity. Soon, AI may write new programs thousands of times faster than humans. A quick Google search reveals that in recorded history, approximately 90 percent of all the scientists who lived throughout history are **alive today**. These modern scientists are processing data often with supercomputers that might have otherwise taken hundreds of years within a matter of minutes! Please make no mistake: AI is here to stay and is already making itself at home through big corporations that serve the masses.

How many AIs are out there?

More than 4 billion devices already have AI-powered assistants, which is set to reach 8.4 billion by 2024. Nearly half of Americans use digital assistants—42% on their smartphones, 14% on a computer or tablet, and 8% on a standalone device such as Amazon Echo or Google Home.

These changes will kick several megatrends into high gear, and you're going along for the ride whether

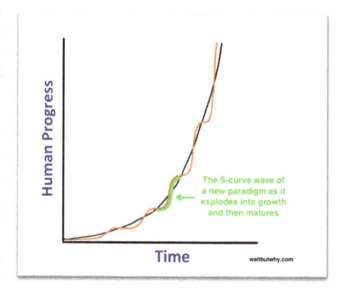

you like it! Or not! Technology has already changed the world as we know it within the last 50 years. Now, technology is ramping up into high gear, further accelerating change.

I believe the future is bright as long as we keep the technology out of the hands of the maniacs who want to rule the world.

The evolution of AI is essentially the evolution of human progress. It is not just the speed at which data is processed but the rate that technology is evolving. With computers writing their own algorithms and programming code, it creates an exponential acceleration rate. "The new electricity", as per Doctor Andrew NG, will transform society as we now know it today.

ChatGPT reached one million users faster than any other online application.

Amount of time to reach one million users for online applications:

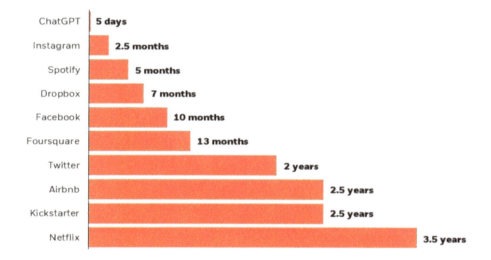

Source: Statista, with data from company announcements via Business Insider/LinkedIn, as of January 24, 2023. Kickstarter measured as one million backers, Airbnb measured as one million nights booked, Instagram measured as one million downloads.

Some people call this artificial intelligence, but the reality is this technology will enhance us. So instead of artificial intelligence, I think we'll augment our intelligence.

Ginni Rometty

What Is AI Exactly?

Intelligence (AI) is a broad field of computer science focused on creating machines and systems that can perform tasks that typically require human intelligence. These tasks include problem-solving, learning from experience, understanding natural language, recognizing patterns, making decisions, and adapting to new situations. AI aims to develop algorithms and systems that can replicate or simulate human-like cognitive functions.

There are two primary categories of AI:

1. **Narrow AI (or Weak AI)** refers to AI systems designed and trained for specific tasks or domains. These systems excel at performing well-defined tasks but lack general intelligence or the ability to transfer their skills to unrelated tasks. Examples of narrow AI include virtual personal assistants like Siri and Alexa, image recognition software, and recommendation algorithms used by streaming platforms.
2. **General AI (or Strong AI):** General AI, also known as artificial general intelligence (AGI), is a form of AI that possesses human-like intellect and the ability to understand, learn, and apply knowledge across a wide range of tasks and domains. AGI could reason, plan, solve problems, and adapt to new and unfamiliar situations. Achieving AGI remains a long-term goal and is an area of active research in AI. Still, it has not been realized as of September 2023.

AI encompasses various subfields and techniques:

- **Machine Learning (ML):** ML is a subset of AI that focuses on developing algorithms that can learn from data. It includes supervised learning, unsupervised learning, and reinforcement learning.
- **Deep Learning:** Deep learning is a type of ML that uses artificial neural networks with multiple layers (deep neural networks) to model and solve complex problems, often achieving state-of-the-art results in tasks like image and speech recognition.
- **Natural Language Processing (NLP):** NLP enables machines to understand, interpret, and generate human language. It is essential for chatbots, language translation, and sentiment analysis applications.
- **Computer Vision:** Computer vision focuses on teaching computers to interpret and understand visual information from the world, allowing them to recognize objects, scenes, and emotions from images and videos.
- **Reinforcement Learning:** This type of learning involves training agents to make sequences of decisions to maximize a reward, often used in applications like game playing and robotics.

AI has applications in various domains, including healthcare, finance, autonomous vehicles, robotics, recommendation systems, etc. It continues to advance and has the potential to significantly impact numerous aspects of society, from improving healthcare and optimizing industries to enhancing our daily lives through smart devices and services.

The pace of progress in artificial intelligence (I'm not referring to narrow AI) is incredibly fast. Unless you have direct exposure to groups like DeepMind, you have no idea how fast—it is growing at a pace close to exponential. The risk of something seriously dangerous happening is in the five-year time frame. 10 years at most.

Elon Musk wrote in a comment on Edge.org

What Is the Current State of AI?

1. **Profound Learning Dominance:** Deep learning, a subset of machine learning, continued to dominate AI research and applications. Deep neural networks were used in a wide range of applications, including image and speech recognition, natural language processing, and autonomous systems.

2. **Natural Language Processing (NLP) Advancements:** NLP made significant strides with models like GPT-3 (Generative Pre-trained Transformer 3) and BERT (Bidirectional Encoder Representations from Transformers). These models demonstrated remarkable language understanding and generation capabilities.

3. **Computer Vision Breakthroughs:** Computer vision technologies advanced, enabling tasks such as object detection, image segmentation, and facial recognition to achieve unprecedented accuracy and efficiency. Autonomous vehicles and drones benefited from these advancements.

4. **AI in Healthcare:** AI played a growing role in healthcare, aiding in diagnostics, drug discovery, and patient care. AI models were used to analyze medical images, predict disease outcomes, and assist in personalized treatment plans.

5. **AI Ethics and Fairness:** Concerns about AI ethics and fairness gained prominence. Efforts were made to address issues related to bias in AI algorithms, data privacy, and the responsible use of AI in various industries.

6. **AI in Business:** AI adoption in businesses continued to increase, with applications in customer service, marketing, supply chain management, and finance. AI-driven chatbots, recommendation systems, and predictive analytics became more common.

7. **Autonomous Systems:** Progress was made in developing autonomous systems, including self-driving cars, drones, and robots. These technologies aimed to enhance safety and efficiency in transportation, delivery, and manufacturing.

8. **AI Research and Open-Source Tools:** The AI research community remained active, and numerous open-source AI frameworks and libraries (e.g., TensorFlow, PyTorch) continued to facilitate AI development and experimentation.

9. **AI and Pandemic Response:** AI was applied in various ways to address challenges posed by the COVID-19 pandemic. This included using AI for epidemiological modeling, drug discovery, and contact tracing.

10. **Quantum Computing and AI:** Quantum computing research intersected with AI as scientists explored the potential for quantum algorithms to accelerate machine learning tasks.

11. **AI Regulation and Policy:** Governments and organizations began to develop and implement regulations and policies related to AI, aiming to ensure its responsible and ethical use.

12. **AI for Climate Change:** AI was leveraged to address environmental challenges, including climate modeling, resource management, and energy optimization.

It's important to keep in mind that the field of AI is highly dynamic, and new developments continue to emerge at a rapid pace. AI's potential applications and impact on various industries are expected to grow significantly in the coming years, with ongoing advancements in technology and research.

The development of full artificial intelligence could spell the end of the human race… It would take off on its own, and redesign itself at an ever-increasing rate. Humans, who are limited by slow biological evolution, couldn't compete, and would be superseded.

Stephen Hawking told the BBC

What Are the Most Significant New Evolving Trends in AI?

Several emerging trends are shaping the field of artificial intelligence (AI). Here are some of the biggest evolving trends in AI:

1. **AI in Edge Computing**: Edge AI involves deploying AI models directly on edge devices (e.g., smartphones, IoT devices) rather than relying solely on cloud-based processing. This trend was gaining momentum to enable faster, more efficient, and privacy-aware AI applications at the edge of networks.

2. **Responsible AI and Ethical AI:** A growing emphasis was on responsible AI practices and ethical considerations. Organizations and researchers were developing guidelines and frameworks for ensuring fairness, transparency, and accountability in AI systems.

3. **AI Explainability and Interpretability:** As AI models become more complex, the need for understanding and explaining their decisions increases. Research and development efforts were focused on creating interpretable AI models and techniques to explain AI reasoning.

4. **AI in Healthcare Transformation:** AI played a pivotal role in healthcare, with applications ranging from medical image analysis and drug discovery to personalized treatment plans and telemedicine. The COVID-19 pandemic accelerated the adoption of AI in healthcare.

5. **AI in Natural Language Processing (NLP):** Developing increasingly sophisticated NLP models was ongoing. Researchers were improving language understanding, generation, and translation capabilities, leading to more natural and context-aware AI interactions.

6. **AI in Robotics:** Robotics and AI converged, leading to advanced robotics systems with greater autonomy and adaptability. This trend was particularly relevant in manufacturing, healthcare, and agriculture.

7. **AI in Climate Change Mitigation:** AI was leveraged to address climate change challenges. AI models were used for climate modeling, weather forecasting, energy optimization, and environmental monitoring.

8. **Quantum Computing and AI:** Quantum computing was explored to accelerate AI algorithms, particularly for solving complex optimization and machine learning tasks. Quantum AI research was gaining traction.

9. **AI in Financial Services:** The financial industry continued to adopt AI for applications such as fraud detection, risk assessment, algorithmic trading, and customer service automation.

10. **AI and Augmented Reality (AR):** AI-powered AR applications are becoming more prevalent, enhancing user experiences in gaming, education, and enterprise.

11. **AI-Enhanced Creativity:** AI tools and algorithms were being developed to assist and augment human creativity in art, music composition, content generation, and design.

12. **AI Regulation and Standards:** Governments and regulatory bodies worked on AI regulations and standards to ensure responsible and ethical AI development and deployment.

13. **AI in Cybersecurity:** AI bolsters cybersecurity efforts by identifying and mitigating threats, detecting anomalies, and improving overall security measures.

14. **AI in Education:** AI-driven personalized learning platforms and educational tools were being developed to adapt to students' needs and optimize educational outcomes.

15. **AI and Biotechnology:** AI plays a significant role in biotechnology, aiding in genomics research, drug discovery, and the development of personalized medicine.

16. **AI and Retail**: Retailers used AI for inventory management, demand forecasting, customer analytics, and personalized shopping experiences.

Artificial intelligence is not a substitute for human intelligence: it is a tool to amplify human creativity and ingenuity.

Fei Fei Li

What Is AI Changing First in the World?

Artificial Intelligence (AI) is transforming various aspects of the world, and its impact can be observed in several areas. While the specific changes AI is bringing about may vary by industry and region, here are some of the areas that AI is significantly changing first in the world:

1. **Healthcare:** AI is revolutionizing healthcare by improving diagnostic accuracy, streamlining administrative tasks, and enabling personalized treatment plans. AI-powered tools are assisting medical professionals in tasks like medical image analysis, drug discovery, and patient care.

2. **Finance:** In the financial sector, AI is being used for fraud detection, algorithmic trading, credit risk assessment, and customer service automation. AI-driven chatbots and robo-advisors are changing how financial services are delivered.

3. **Manufacturing:** AI-powered automation is transforming manufacturing processes. Robots and smart machines equipped with AI are enhancing production efficiency, quality control, and predictive maintenance.

4. **Retail:** Retailers are using AI for inventory management, demand forecasting, and personalized customer experiences. AI-driven recommendation systems provide customers with tailored product suggestions.

5. **Customer Service:** AI chatbots and virtual assistants are changing the landscape of customer service. They provide quick and efficient responses to customer inquiries, improving the overall customer experience.

6. **Transportation:** Self-driving cars, trucks, and drones are examples of AI technologies that are reshaping transportation. AI is also being used for route optimization, traffic management, and predictive maintenance in the logistics sector.

7. **Education:** AI is making education more personalized and accessible. AI-powered educational platforms adapt to individual student needs, and virtual tutors help with homework and learning challenges.

8. **Energy and Sustainability:** AI is used to optimize energy consumption, improve grid management, and increase the efficiency of renewable energy sources. It plays a role in monitoring and reducing environmental impact.

9. **Entertainment:** AI-driven content recommendation systems are prevalent in streaming services, suggesting movies, music, and TV shows based on user preferences. AI is also used in video game design and graphics rendering.

10. **Agriculture:** Precision agriculture is benefiting from AI technologies that analyze data from sensors, drones, and satellites to optimize crop management, irrigation, and yield predictions.

11. **Security and Surveillance:** AI is enhancing security through facial recognition, anomaly detection, and predictive analytics. It's used in airports, public spaces, and online platforms to improve safety and protect against cyber threats.

12. **Language Translation:** AI-powered translation services are breaking down language barriers, facilitating communication across borders and cultures.

13. **Research and Development:** AI accelerates research in various fields, such as drug discovery, materials science, and astronomy. AI algorithms analyze vast datasets and simulate experiments, leading to scientific breakthroughs.

14. **Urban Planning:** AI contributes to smarter city planning by optimizing traffic flow, energy usage, waste management, and public services.
15. **Telecommunications:** AI is improving network performance, predicting network issues, and optimizing data routing in telecommunications networks.

These are just a few examples of how AI is changing the world across different sectors. The transformative power of AI lies in its ability to analyze vast amounts of data, make predictions, automate tasks, and enhance decision-making across a wide range of industries and applications. AI's impact is likely to continue expanding as technology evolves and new AI applications emerge.

The key to artificial intelligence has always been the representation.

Jeff Hawkins

What Are the Biggest Benefits
of AI Short and Long Term?

Artificial Intelligence (AI) offers a wide range of benefits in both the short and long term, which can have profound impacts on various aspects of society. Here are some of the biggest benefits:

Short-Term Benefits:

1. **Automation:** AI can automate repetitive and mundane tasks, freeing up human workers to focus on more creative and complex tasks. This can increase efficiency and productivity in various industries.
2. **Data Analysis:** AI can quickly analyze vast amounts of data, providing valuable insights for businesses, healthcare, and research.
3. **Personalization:** AI algorithms can tailor products, services, and content to individual preferences, leading to better customer experiences and increased engagement.
4. **Cost Reduction:** Automation and optimization through AI can lead to significant cost savings for businesses, as it reduces the need for human labor and minimizes errors.
5. **Improved Healthcare:** AI can assist in early disease detection, drug discovery, and the personalization of treatment plans, ultimately improving patient outcomes and reducing healthcare costs.
6. **Enhanced Cybersecurity:** AI can be used to identify and respond to cybersecurity threats in real time, helping to protect sensitive data and systems.
7. **Long-Term Benefits:**
8. **Scientific Advancements:** AI can accelerate scientific research and discovery in fields such as physics, chemistry, and biology, potentially leading to breakthroughs in understanding and solving complex problems.
9. **Sustainable Solutions:** AI can help optimize resource usage and develop sustainable solutions for environmental challenges, including climate change, energy conservation, and natural resource management.
10. **Space Exploration:** AI can play a crucial role in advancing space exploration by autonomously controlling spacecraft, analyzing data from distant planets, and enabling long-duration missions.
11. **Improved Education:** AI-powered personalized learning platforms can provide tailored education experiences, helping students of all levels reach their full potential.
12. **Assistive Technologies:** AI-driven assistive technologies can enhance the quality of life for individuals with disabilities, improving accessibility and independence.
13. **Economic Growth:** The widespread adoption of AI can lead to the creation of new industries and job opportunities, stimulating economic growth.
14. **Healthcare Transformation:** Long-term benefits include AI-driven advancements in predictive medicine, brain-computer interfaces, and the potential for personalized healthcare at an unprecedented level.
15. **Ethical and Safety Advances:** Ongoing research into AI ethics and safety can lead to the development of responsible AI systems that minimize bias, adhere to ethical principles, and ensure safety.

It's important to note that while AI offers significant advantages, it also comes with challenges and risks, such as job displacement, ethical concerns, and potential misuse. Managing these challenges and harnessing AI's potential for the benefit of humanity will be important as we continue to integrate AI into various aspects of our lives.

It's going to be interesting to see how society deals with artificial intelligence, but it will definitely be cool.

Colin Angle

What Is the Timeline for AI-Driven Change

The timeline for AI-driven change is challenging to predict with precision because it depends on various factors, including technological advancements, regulatory developments, societal acceptance, and economic conditions. However, I can provide a general overview of how AI-driven change has been unfolding and might continue to evolve in the coming years:

1. **Past Developments (Up to 2021):** AI has been advancing rapidly over the past decade. Major breakthroughs, such as deep learning, have significantly improved AI's capabilities. Industries like healthcare, finance, and manufacturing have already witnessed substantial AI-driven changes. Chatbots, recommendation systems, and image recognition technologies are common examples of AI applications that are now integrated into daily life.

2. **Short-Term (2021–2025):** In the near term, we can expect continued growth in AI adoption across industries. AI-driven automation will streamline operations in manufacturing, logistics, and customer service. AI in healthcare will become more personalized, with advancements in diagnostics and treatment recommendations. Self-driving cars and drones may become more common, although widespread adoption may still face regulatory challenges.

3. **Mid-Term (2025–2035):** Over the next decade or so, we may see further AI integration into urban planning, transportation, and energy management. AI could play a significant role in addressing environmental challenges, such as climate change and resource optimization. AI in education may transform the way students learn, with personalized curricula and virtual tutors.

4. **Long-Term (Beyond 2035):** In the long term, AI-driven change may become even more profound. We may witness the emergence of highly advanced AI systems capable of complex decision-making, creative tasks, and scientific discovery. AI ethics and regulation may evolve to address the ethical and societal implications of AI. Quantum computing and AI integration could lead to exponential advancements in AI capabilities.

5. **Unknown Variables:** It's important to note that unexpected breakthroughs or disruptions can significantly alter the AI timeline. Regulatory developments, societal concerns, and economic factors can also influence the pace of AI-driven change. Additionally, the adoption of AI may vary by region and industry, resulting in uneven progress.

6. **Ethical and Regulatory Considerations:** As AI becomes more integrated into society, ethical considerations and regulatory frameworks will likely become increasingly important. Balancing technological advancement with ethical and responsible AI practices will be a key challenge.

7. **AI in Research and Development:** AI-driven research and development may accelerate scientific discoveries in various fields, potentially leading to innovations and solutions to pressing global challenges.

It's important to approach AI-driven change with a focus on responsible and ethical AI development. Ensuring transparency, fairness, and accountability in AI systems will be essential for achieving positive outcomes and addressing potential challenges.

While this timeline provides a general overview, the specific trajectory of AI-driven change may vary across industries and regions. Continuous monitoring of AI developments, staying informed about regulatory changes, and adapting to evolving technology trends will be crucial for individuals, organizations, and policymakers.

Some people worry that artificial intelligence will make us feel inferior, but then, anybody in his right mind should have an inferiority complex every time he looks at a flower.

Alan Kay

Who Will Be Affected Most by AI Changes in the World?

The impact of AI changes will be felt across various sectors and demographics, but the extent and nature of the effects may vary significantly. Here are some groups and sectors that may be particularly affected by AI changes in the world:

1. **Workers in Certain Industries:** Jobs that involve routine and repetitive tasks are more susceptible to automation by AI. Industries like manufacturing, customer service, and data entry may experience workforce disruptions. Workers in these sectors may need to acquire new skills to remain employable.

2. **Low-Skilled and Middle-Skilled Workers:** Jobs that require lower to moderate levels of skill may face challenges due to automation. These workers may need retraining or upskilling to transition to roles that complement AI technologies.

3. **High-Skilled Professionals:** Even high-skilled professionals are not immune to AI-driven changes. AI can augment the work of doctors, lawyers, researchers, and financial analysts. Professionals in these fields may see changes in their job roles and the tasks they perform.

4. **Education Sector:** The education sector may be transformed by AI, particularly in personalized learning and online education. Teachers and educators may need to adapt to AI-driven tools and methodologies.

5. **Healthcare Professionals:** AI is already making inroads in healthcare, aiding in diagnostics, treatment planning, and patient care. Healthcare professionals will need to collaborate with AI systems and maintain expertise in their fields.

6. **Elderly and Vulnerable Populations:** AI technologies can be used to provide better care for the elderly and vulnerable populations. This demographic may benefit from AI-driven solutions in healthcare, caregiving, and home assistance.

7. **Small and Medium-sized Enterprises (SMEs):** SMEs may face challenges in adopting AI due to resource constraints. However, AI can also provide cost-effective solutions for small businesses, such as chatbots for customer support and data analytics for decision-making.

8. **Developing Countries:** The impact of AI may vary by region, and developing countries may face challenges in adopting and benefiting from AI technologies. Bridging the digital divide and ensuring equitable access to AI tools will be important.

9. **Ethical and Regulatory Bodies:** Policymakers, regulators, and ethicists will play a crucial role in shaping the responsible development and deployment of AI. They will need to address ethical concerns, data privacy issues, and establish regulatory frameworks.

10. **Consumers:** Consumers will experience the effects of AI changes through products and services that incorporate AI features. These include AI-driven recommendations, virtual assistants, and personalized experiences in areas like e-commerce and entertainment.

11. **Researchers and Innovators:** AI researchers and innovators will continue to drive advancements in the field. Their work will influence how AI technologies are developed and applied across industries.

12. **Environmental Sector:** AI can be used to address environmental challenges, such as climate modeling, resource optimization, and conservation efforts. Environmentalists and policymakers may rely on AI to inform sustainability initiatives.

It's important to note that AI changes can bring both opportunities and challenges. While certain jobs and industries may undergo transformations, new roles and industries related to AI development, implementation, and oversight may emerge. To mitigate potential negative effects and harness the benefits of AI, there is a growing emphasis on reskilling and upskilling, responsible AI development, and ethical considerations in AI deployment. Additionally, governments, organizations, and educational institutions are taking steps to ensure that AI benefits are distributed more equitably across society.

There is no reason and no way that a human mind can keep up with an artificial intelligence machine by 2035.

Gray Scott

Who Will Be Affected Least
in the World by AI?

While AI has the potential to impact various sectors and demographics worldwide, certain groups and industries may be less directly affected or less susceptible to immediate disruption by AI-driven changes. Here are some groups and sectors that may be relatively less affected by AI:

1. **Highly Specialized Professions:** Professions that require a high degree of creativity, emotional Intelligence, or complex problem-solving may be less susceptible to AI automation. These include artists, musicians, psychologists, and some research scientists.
2. **Skilled Trades:** Skilled trades, such as plumbers, electricians, and mechanics, involve hands-on work that is difficult to automate fully. These jobs often require a deep understanding of physical systems and components.
3. **Human-Centric Services:** Roles that involve human interaction, empathy, and personalized care, such as therapists, social workers, and counselors, may be less directly impacted by AI. While AI can assist in some aspects, the human touch remains essential.
4. **Creativity and Innovation:** Industries focused on creativity, innovation, and design, such as fashion, architecture, and product design, rely on unique human insights and artistic expression that are challenging for AI to replicate fully.
5. **Education and Training:** Teachers and educators, particularly those who emphasize critical thinking, problem-solving, and mentorship, play a vital role in preparing individuals for the changing workforce. While AI can support education, human educators remain essential.
6. **Entrepreneurship:** Entrepreneurs and business leaders who innovate and create new markets may be less affected by AI. These individuals are often at the forefront of leveraging AI for business growth.
7. **Community and Social Services:** Jobs in community development, social work, and nonprofit organizations involve a strong human element, addressing complex and context-specific social issues.
8. **Legal and Ethical Fields:** Legal and ethical experts are needed to navigate the complex challenges posed by AI, including issues related to liability, ethics, and regulations.
9. **Diverse and Niche Markets:** Some niche markets and specialized industries may have limited AI application due to the uniqueness and specificity of their products or services.
10. **Primary Industries:** Industries related to agriculture, forestry, and fishing, which involve outdoor and hands-on work, may have limited AI application beyond specific tasks like crop monitoring.
11. **Cultural Preservation:** Roles related to cultural preservation, such as archivists, historians, and museum curators, require a deep understanding of historical and cultural context, making them less prone to automation.

It's important to note that even in less AI-affected areas, AI may still play a complementary role. For example, professionals in these sectors may leverage AI tools for data analysis, research support, or administrative tasks. Additionally, AI's influence can indirectly impact various aspects of society, such as regulations, consumer preferences, and global economic trends.

The extent to which AI affects different groups and sectors will depend on the rate of AI adoption, technological advancements, and how well individuals and organizations adapt to the changing landscape. Continuous learning and adaptability remain valuable skills in an AI-driven world.

Artificial intelligence will reach human levels by around 2029. Follow that out further to, say, 2045, we will have multiplied the intelligence, the human biological machine intelligence of our civilization a billion-fold.

Ray Kurzweil

What AI Opportunities Lie in Future Changes for Business People Regarding Upcoming Trends?

The evolving trends in artificial intelligence (AI) present numerous opportunities for businesspeople and entrepreneurs. As AI technologies continue to advance, there are several key opportunities for individuals and businesses to explore:

1. **AI-Driven Business Models:** Consider integrating AI into your existing business models or developing new models that leverage AI capabilities. This might involve offering AI-based products or services, such as AI-driven software solutions, chatbots, or personalized recommendations.

2. **Data-Driven Decision-Making:** Harness the power of AI to make data-driven decisions. AI algorithms can analyze vast amounts of data to provide insights into customer behavior, market trends, and operational efficiencies. This can inform strategic planning and improve business outcomes.

3. **AI in Customer Experience:** Enhance customer experiences by implementing AI-powered chatbots, virtual assistants, and recommendation engines. These technologies can provide personalized interactions, streamline customer support, and boost engagement.

4. **Automation and Efficiency:** Automate repetitive and time-consuming tasks within your business processes using AI-driven automation tools. This can free up human resources for more strategic and creative tasks.

5. **AI-Enhanced Marketing:** Use AI for more effective marketing campaigns. AI can optimize ad targeting, content creation, and A/B testing, leading to improved ROI in marketing efforts.

6. **E-commerce and Retail:** Embrace AI in e-commerce and retail to enhance the shopping experience. AI-driven recommendation engines can increase cross-selling and upselling opportunities. Implementing visual search and augmented reality can also engage customers in new ways.

7. **AI in Supply Chain Management:** Optimize your supply chain with AI-driven forecasting, demand prediction, and inventory management. AI can help reduce costs, improve efficiency, and enhance responsiveness to market changes.

8. **Healthcare and Wellness Tech:** Explore opportunities in the rapidly growing healthcare and wellness tech sectors. AI applications include telemedicine, remote patient monitoring, and predictive analytics for disease prevention.

9. **Financial Services:** Develop AI-driven solutions for financial services, such as robo-advisors, fraud detection systems, and credit scoring models. These solutions can cater to a wide range of financial needs.

10. **AI-Driven Content Creation:** AI can assist in content creation, whether in writing articles, generating marketing materials, or producing creative works. Explore AI-powered content generation tools to streamline content production.

11. **AI Consulting and Services:** If you have expertise in AI, consider offering consulting and services to businesses looking to integrate AI into their operations. This could include AI strategy development, implementation, and training.

12. **AI for Sustainability:** Explore AI applications for sustainability and environmental protection. Businesses that develop AI solutions to address environmental challenges, such as energy optimization and conservation, may find opportunities in this growing field.

13. **AI and Education:** Develop AI-driven educational tools, platforms, or content that cater to personalized learning and skill development. Online education and edtech platforms are areas with significant growth potential.

14. **AI for Small and Medium-sized Enterprises (SMEs):** SMEs may require guidance and support in adopting AI. Provide services or solutions tailored to the needs and budgets of smaller businesses.

15. **AI Ethics and Governance:** As AI adoption grows, there is a need for ethical AI practices and governance. Businesspeople with expertise in AI ethics and compliance may find opportunities in guiding responsible AI development.

It's important to keep in mind that successful AI ventures often require collaboration, access to data, and a deep understanding of both AI technology and the specific industry or domain you are targeting. Additionally, staying updated with AI trends and fostering a culture of innovation within your organization can be instrumental in seizing AI opportunities.

You have to talk about "The Terminator" if you're talking about artificial intelligence. I actually think that that's way off. I don't think that an artificially intelligent system that has superhuman intelligence will be violent. I do think that it will disrupt our culture.

Gray Scott

What Does the Future Look Like Living with AI?

The future of living with artificial intelligence (AI) promises to be transformative and filled with both opportunities and challenges. While predicting the exact details of the future is challenging, we can envision some key aspects of what living with AI might look like:

1. **Enhanced Convenience and Efficiency:** AI will continue to make our lives more convenient and efficient. Smart homes equipped with AI-driven systems will automate tasks, control energy consumption, and enhance security. AI-powered virtual assistants will manage our schedules, answer questions, and provide personalized recommendations.

2. **Personalized Experiences:** AI will tailor our experiences in various domains. In entertainment, AI will suggest movies, music, and books based on our preferences. In healthcare, AI will offer personalized treatment plans and wellness recommendations. Shopping experiences will become more personalized with AI-driven product recommendations.

3. **Health and Wellness:** AI will play a significant role in healthcare and wellness. AI-powered wearable devices will monitor our health, detect anomalies, and provide early warnings. Telemedicine and AI-driven diagnostics will make healthcare more accessible and efficient.

4. **Education and Learning:** AI will transform education by providing personalized learning experiences. AI tutors and adaptive learning platforms will cater to individual student needs, helping learners of all ages acquire new skills and knowledge.

5. **AI-Enhanced Work:** AI will augment the workforce rather than replace it. In the workplace, AI will automate routine tasks, allowing employees to focus on more creative and strategic responsibilities. Collaboration with AI tools and algorithms will become commonplace.

6. **Transportation:** Autonomous vehicles, including self-driving cars, trucks, and drones, will change the way we travel and transport goods. Commutes may become more productive or leisurely as AI takes over driving tasks.

7. **AI and Creativity:** AI will assist in creative endeavors such as art, music, and content creation. Artists and musicians will collaborate with AI-generated content, leading to new forms of artistic expression.

8. **Ethical and Regulatory Considerations:** As AI becomes more integrated into society, ethical and regulatory discussions will become increasingly important. Ensuring AI fairness, transparency, accountability, and data privacy will be key considerations.

9. **AI in Decision-Making:** AI will provide insights and recommendations for decision-making across various industries. In healthcare, AI may assist in clinical decisions. In finance, AI-driven algorithms will inform investment choices.

10. **AI and Social Interactions:** AI-powered chatbots and virtual assistants will become more conversational and assistive in daily life. AI-driven language translation will facilitate global communication.

11. **AI and Sustainability:** AI will be harnessed to address global challenges, including climate change. AI models will assist in climate modeling, resource management, and sustainable practices.

12. **Continuous Learning:** Staying up-to-date with AI technology and adapting to new AI-driven tools and platforms will become essential for individuals and organizations.

13. **Economic Impact:** AI will influence job markets and industries, leading to shifts in employment and skills demand. Adaptation and reskilling will be necessary for individuals to thrive in the AI-driven economy.

14. **AI-Generated Innovation:** AI will contribute to scientific discoveries and innovations across various fields, potentially accelerating progress in areas like healthcare, materials science, and energy.

15. **AI Assistance for Aging Populations:** AI-driven healthcare and caregiving solutions will assist elderly populations in maintaining independence and well-being as they age.

It's important to note that the future of living with AI will be shaped by collective decisions related to ethics, regulations, and responsible AI development. Embracing AI's potential while addressing its challenges will be critical in ensuring that AI enhances our lives and contributes to a better future.

A year spent in artificial intelligence is enough to make one believe in God.

Alan Perlis

What Are Some of the AI Advancements in Healthcare?

AI has made significant advancements in healthcare, offering the potential to transform the industry in various ways. Some notable AI advancements in healthcare include:

1. **Medical Imaging Interpretation:** AI algorithms can analyze medical images such as X-rays, MRIs, and CT scans to detect abnormalities and assist healthcare professionals in diagnosing conditions like cancer, fractures, and neurological disorders with higher accuracy and speed.

2. **Early Disease Detection:** AI models can identify early signs of diseases by analyzing patient data, enabling early intervention and improved outcomes. For example, AI can predict the risk of heart disease or diabetes based on patient records.

3. **Drug Discovery and Development:** AI-powered simulations and analysis of molecular data can significantly accelerate drug discovery and development processes, potentially reducing the time and cost required to bring new medications to market.

4. **Personalized Treatment Plans:** AI can analyze patient data, including genetic information, to create personalized treatment plans that are tailored to an individual's unique characteristics and needs, increasing the likelihood of treatment success.

5. **Clinical Decision Support:** AI systems can assist healthcare providers by offering diagnostic suggestions, treatment recommendations, and risk assessments, reducing the likelihood of medical errors and improving patient care.

6. **Health Monitoring:** Wearable devices equipped with AI can continuously monitor vital signs, activity levels, and other health metrics, providing real-time data to patients and healthcare providers for proactive health management.

7. **Natural Language Processing (NLP):** NLP algorithms can analyze electronic health records, transcribe doctor-patient conversations, and extract valuable information from unstructured text, making it easier to manage patient information and conduct research.

8. **Telemedicine and Remote Monitoring:** AI-driven telehealth platforms enable remote consultations, making healthcare more accessible, especially in rural or underserved areas. Remote monitoring devices can also alert healthcare providers to potential issues.

9. **Robot-Assisted Surgery:** AI-powered robotic systems assist surgeons in performing complex procedures with greater precision and control, reducing the risk of complications and shortening recovery times.

10. **Drug Adverse Event Monitoring:** AI can sift through massive volumes of healthcare data to identify potential adverse events related to medications, helping regulatory agencies and healthcare providers monitor drug safety.

11. **Healthcare Fraud Detection:** AI can analyze insurance claims and billing data to detect fraudulent activities, helping to reduce healthcare costs and improve the integrity of the healthcare system.

12. **Epidemiological Surveillance:** AI can analyze data from various sources, including social media, to monitor and predict disease outbreaks, enabling early intervention and containment measures.

These AI advancements have the potential to improve patient care, increase the efficiency of healthcare delivery, reduce costs, and ultimately save lives. However, they also come with challenges related to data privacy, regulatory compliance, and ethical considerations, which need to be carefully addressed as AI continues to play a larger role in healthcare.

In our business, we talk about emerging technologies and how they impact society. We've never seen a technology move as fast as AI has to impact society and technology. This is by far the fastest moving technology that we've ever tracked in terms of its impact and we're just getting started.

Paul Daugherty

What Are the Secrets to Future Success in an AI World?

Succeeding in an AI-driven world requires a combination of skills, strategies, and adaptability. Here are some "secrets" to future success in a world influenced by artificial intelligence:

1. **Continuous Learning and Adaptability:**
    *   Embrace a growth mindset and be open to learning new skills throughout your life.
    *   Stay updated with the latest AI trends and technologies, as they are continually evolving.
    *   Be adaptable and willing to pivot when necessary as industries and job roles change due to AI.
2. **AI Literacy:**
    *   Develop a basic understanding of AI principles, terminologies, and its applications across industries.
    *   Familiarize yourself with AI tools and platforms relevant to your field.
3. **Data Literacy:**
    *   Understand the importance of data in AI and how to work with data effectively.
    *   Develop data analysis skills to extract meaningful insights from data.
4. **Problem-Solving and Critical Thinking:**
    *   Cultivate strong problem-solving and critical thinking skills, as AI often assists in decision-making but may not replace human judgment entirely.
    *   Learn to identify and frame problems that AI can help solve.
5. **Creativity and Innovation:**
    *   Leverage your creativity to find novel solutions and ideas that complement AI technologies.
    *   Embrace innovation and explore opportunities for AI-driven innovation in your industry.
6. **Ethical Considerations:**
    *   Understand the ethical implications of AI and the responsible use of AI in your field.
    *   Advocate for ethical AI practices within your organization or industry.
7. **Collaboration and Teamwork:**
    *   Collaborate effectively with AI systems and other professionals, as cross functional teams often produce the best results.
    *   Develop strong interpersonal and communication skills.
8. **Entrepreneurial Mindset:**
    *   Explore entrepreneurial opportunities in AI, such as developing AI-powered products or services.
    *   Be willing to take calculated risks and innovate in your career or business.
9. **AI-Enhanced Productivity:**
    *   Utilize AI tools to enhance your productivity. For example, use AI-driven assistants for scheduling and data analysis.
    *   Automate routine tasks to free up time for more strategic work.
10. **Embrace Lifelong Learning:**
    *   Invest in ongoing education and professional development, including online courses, workshops, and certifications related to AI and relevant skills.
    *   Seek mentorship and guidance from AI experts or professionals in your field.

11. **Global Perspective:**
    - Understand the global impact of AI and its implications for various regions and industries.
    - Explore international opportunities and collaborations in AI-related fields.

12. **Resilience and Adaptation:**
    - Develop resilience to navigate changes and uncertainties in the AI landscape.
    - Be prepared to adapt to shifting job roles and industry dynamics.

13. **AI Advocacy and Policy Engagement:**
    - Engage in discussions about AI policy and regulations, advocating for responsible AI use and ethical considerations.
    - Stay informed about AI-related policies and developments that may affect your industry.

14. **Networking and Community Engagement:**
    - Build a strong professional network, including AI experts and professionals in your field.
    - Participate in AI communities and industry associations to stay connected and informed.

15. **Balance Technology with Humanity:**
    - Recognize that while AI can enhance productivity and decision-making, it's essential to balance technology with human values, empathy, and ethical considerations.

Success in an AI-driven world is not solely about technical skills but also about the ability to collaborate, innovate, and adapt to a rapidly changing landscape. By combining technical proficiency with creativity and a commitment to ethical AI practices, individuals and organizations can thrive in the AI era.

According to Investors: "the next wave of AI startups would enable developers to construct applications using AI models and integrate them with external data sources".

Humans need and want more time to interact with each other. I think AI coming about and replacing routine jobs is pushing us to do what we should be doing anyway: the creation of more humanistic service jobs.

Kai-Fu Lee

What Is the Next Wave of AI Startups?

AI is enabling developers to construct applications using AI models and integrate them with external data sources is centered around simplifying and democratizing the process of building AI-powered applications. This involves two key aspects: AI model construction and data integration.

1. **AI Model Construction:**
   - Accessibility: AI startups aim to make AI models more accessible to developers who may not have deep expertise in machine learning or data science. This is achieved by providing user-friendly tools and platforms that abstract away the complexities of model creation.
   - Pre-trained Models: Many startups offer pre-trained AI models for various tasks like natural language processing (NLP), computer vision, speech recognition, and more. Developers can leverage these models as building blocks for their applications, saving time and effort in training models from scratch.
   - Customization: These platforms allow developers to fine-tune and customize pre-trained models to better suit their specific application needs. Customization can involve training models on domain-specific data or adjusting model parameters.

2. **Integration with External Data Sources:**
   - Data Connectivity: AI startups provide mechanisms for developers to easily connect their AI-powered applications with external data sources. These sources can include databases, APIs, IoT devices, or any other repositories of relevant information.
   - Data Transformation: Startups often offer tools for data preprocessing and transformation. This ensures that data from external sources is in a format that AI models can understand and use effectively.
   - Real-time Updates: Some startups focus on real-time data integration, allowing applications to constantly adapt and make predictions based on the most recent data from external sources.

3. **Key Benefits:**
   - Rapid Development: By providing pre-built AI models and simplifying the integration of external data, these startups accelerate the development cycle for AI applications.
   - Reduced Expertise Barrier: Developers with limited AI expertise can leverage these platforms to incorporate AI capabilities into their projects without needing in-depth knowledge of machine learning algorithms.
   - Scalability: Startups often offer scalable infrastructure and cloud-based services, allowing applications to handle increasing data volumes and user loads.
   - Interoperability: The ability to integrate with various external data sources enhances the versatility and functionality of AI applications, making them more valuable in a broader range of use cases.

4. **Use Cases:**
   - Chatbots and Virtual Assistants: Developers can integrate NLP models with external data sources to create conversational AI solutions.

- Predictive Analytics: AI startups enable businesses to build predictive models that utilize both historical and real-time data for forecasting.
- Image and Video Analysis: Computer vision models can be integrated with cameras and image databases for applications in surveillance, healthcare, and more.

In summary, the next wave of AI startups is focused on making AI more accessible and practical for developers by simplifying the process of model construction and enabling seamless integration with external data sources. This democratization of AI technology has the potential to drive innovation across various industries and expand the use of AI-powered applications.

Humane technology starts with an honest appraisal of human nature. We need to do the uncomfortable thing of looking more closely at ourselves.

Tristan Harris

What Is the Simplest Way to Monetize AI?

The simplest way to monetize AI is by offering AI-powered products or services that provide clear value to customers. Here are some straightforward approaches to monetizing AI:

5. **Subscription-based Services:**
   - Develop AI-powered software or platforms and charge customers on a recurring basis for access. This can include AI-driven analytics tools, chatbots, virtual assistants, or data processing services.

6. **Pay-Per-Use or Pay-Per-Transaction:**
   - Charge customers based on their usage of your AI service. For example, you could charge per API call, per document processed, or per prediction made by your AI model.

7. **Licensing AI Models:**
   - Train AI models for specific tasks (e.g., language translation, sentiment analysis) and license them to businesses that require those capabilities. You can charge a fee for the use of your pre-trained models.

8. **Custom AI Development:**
   - Offer AI development services to businesses looking to build custom AI solutions. Charge for the development, deployment, and maintenance of AI models tailored to their specific needs.

1. **Data Monetization:**
   - If you have access to valuable datasets, you can monetize them by offering data analytics, insights, or data-driven decision support services to businesses in need of such information.

2. **AI Consultation and Training:**
   - Provide consultancy services to help businesses implement AI solutions or offer training programs to upskill their teams in AI. Charge fees for your expertise and training materials.

3. **AI-Enhanced Products:**
   - Integrate AI features into existing products or services to enhance their functionality. Charge a premium for the AI-powered features.

4. **SaaS with AI Add-ons:**
   - If you have a software-as-a-service (SaaS) product, consider offering AI add-ons or modules that enhance the capabilities of your base product.
   - Charge separately for these AI enhancements.

5. **AI Marketplaces:**
   - Create a marketplace where AI developers can sell their AI models, algorithms, or applications to a broader user base, and you can take a commission on each sale.

6. **AI-Generated Content:**
   - Develop AI systems that generate creative content, such as articles, images, or music, and monetize this content through advertising, subscriptions, or direct sales.

7. **AI in Healthcare:**
   - In healthcare, you can monetize AI by offering diagnostic or predictive services to healthcare providers or by developing AI-powered medical devices.

8. **AI in Finance:**
   - Develop AI algorithms for financial institutions to optimize trading strategies, risk assessment, or fraud detection, and charge fees for these services.

Successful AI monetization often requires a deep understanding of your target market, a focus on solving real problems, and continuous improvement of your AI capabilities to stay competitive. Additionally, you should consider ethical and privacy concerns when working with AI, as they can impact your monetization strategy and customer trust.

The three big categories [for building ethics into AI] are first, creating an ethical culture; then being transparent; and then finally taking the action of removing exclusion, whether that's in your data sets or your algorithms.

Kathy Baxter

What Kind of Services Help Businesses Implement AI Solutions?

Offering services to help businesses implement AI solutions can be a lucrative business model, as many companies are interested in harnessing the power of artificial intelligence but may lack the in-house expertise to do so effectively. Here are the key services you can provide to assist businesses in implementing AI solutions:

1. **AI Strategy and Assessment:**
   - Begin by conducting an assessment of the client's business needs and goals to determine how AI can benefit them. Develop a comprehensive AI strategy that aligns with their objectives.
2. **Data Analysis and Preparation:**
   - Assist in collecting, cleaning, and preparing the data required for AI model training. This includes data sourcing, data quality assessment, and data transformation.
3. **Custom AI Model Development:**
   - Build custom AI models tailored to the specific needs of the client. This could involve machine learning, deep learning, or other AI techniques, depending on the use case.
4. **AI Model Training and Tuning:**
   - Train and fine-tune AI models to optimize their performance on the client's data. This may involve hyperparameter tuning, feature engineering, and model selection.
5. **Integration with Existing Systems:**
   - Integrate AI solutions seamlessly into the client's existing software infrastructure, whether it's for automating business processes, enhancing customer experiences, or improving decision-making.
6. **Deployment and Monitoring:**
   - Deploy AI models into production environments and set up monitoring systems to ensure that they continue to perform effectively over time. Implement strategies for retraining and maintenance as needed.
7. **Data Security and Privacy Compliance:**
   - Ensure that AI implementations comply with data security and privacy regulations, such as GDPR or HIPAA, and implement best practices for data protection.
8. **User Training and Support:**
   - Provide training sessions and ongoing support to the client's team members who will be using the AI systems. This helps ensure that the technology is effectively utilized.
9. **Performance Metrics and Reporting:**
   - Establish key performance indicators (KPIs) and reporting mechanisms to track the impact of AI on the client's business objectives. Regularly provide insights and reports.
10. **Scalability Planning:**
    - Assist in planning for the scalability of AI solutions as the client's business grows. Ensure that the technology can handle increasing data volumes and user loads.

11. **AI Ethics and Bias Mitigation:**
    - Address ethical considerations and potential biases in AI algorithms. Implement strategies to ensure fairness and transparency in AI decision-making processes.
12. **Cost-Benefit Analysis:**
    - Help the client assess the cost-effectiveness of AI implementation by comparing the benefits gained with the investment made.
13. **AI Roadmap and Future-Proofing:**
    - Develop a roadmap for the client's AI journey, outlining potential future enhancements and upgrades to keep their AI systems competitive.
14. **Regulatory and Compliance Assistance:**
    - Stay up-to-date with AI-related regulations and industry standards and provide guidance to the client to ensure compliance.
15. **AI Vendor Evaluation:**
    - Assist in evaluating third-party AI tools, platforms, or services to determine the best fit for the client's needs if outsourcing is preferred.

Offering a combination of these services can provide comprehensive support to businesses looking to implement AI solutions successfully. As the AI landscape evolves, staying informed about the latest advancements and best practices is crucial to delivering value to your clients.

If we do it right, we might be able to evolve a form of work that taps into our uniquely human capabilities and restores our humanity. The ultimate paradox is that this technology may become a powerful catalyst that we need to reclaim our humanity.

John Hagel

How Is AI Likely to Affect
the Financial System Worldwide?

AI is already having a significant impact on the financial system worldwide, and its influence is expected to continue to grow. Here are several ways AI is likely to affect the financial system:

1. **Improved Customer Experience:**
   - AI-driven chatbots and virtual assistants enhance customer support, providing quick responses to inquiries and resolving issues efficiently.
   - Personalized financial advice and recommendations are made possible through AI algorithms, improving the overall customer experience.

2. **Fraud Detection and Prevention:**
   - AI-powered fraud detection systems can analyze vast amounts of transaction data in real time, identifying suspicious activities and reducing fraudulent transactions.
   - Machine learning models can adapt to evolving fraud patterns, making them more effective in safeguarding financial assets.

3. **Algorithmic Trading and Investment Management:**
   - AI-driven algorithms execute trades and manage investment portfolios with speed and precision, taking advantage of market trends and opportunities.
   - AI-based predictive analytics can assist in making investment decisions by analyzing market data and identifying potential investment targets.

4. **Risk Assessment and Credit Scoring:**
   - AI models assess creditworthiness by analyzing borrowers' financial histories and other relevant data, resulting in more accurate and fair lending decisions.
   - Risk assessment models can provide real-time updates, helping financial institutions manage and mitigate credit risks.

5. **Regulatory Compliance:**
   - AI systems assist financial institutions in complying with complex regulatory requirements by automating data collection, analysis, and reporting.
   - AI can help detect and prevent money laundering and other financial crimes by flagging suspicious transactions.

6. **Algorithmic Trading and Market Liquidity:**
   - AI algorithms contribute to market liquidity by facilitating high-frequency trading and providing liquidity during volatile market conditions.
   - However, AI-driven trading can also contribute to market volatility and flash crashes, necessitating regulatory oversight.

7. **Predictive Analytics and Forecasting:**
   - AI models predict market trends, currency fluctuations, and economic indicators, helping financial professionals make informed decisions.
   - AI can assist in risk modeling and stress testing scenarios to assess the resilience of financial systems.

8. **Cost Reduction and Automation:**
   - AI automation streamlines back-office processes, reducing operational costs for financial institutions.
   - Routine tasks like data entry, reconciliation, and document processing can be automated, freeing up human resources for more strategic roles.

9. **Portfolio Diversification:**
   - AI-driven robo-advisors help retail investors diversify their portfolios based on individual risk profiles and investment goals.
   - This accessibility to diversified portfolios benefits smaller investors who may not have previously had access to wealth management services.

10. **Market Surveillance and Oversight:**
    - Regulators use AI tools for market surveillance to monitor trading activities and identify potential market manipulation or insider trading.
    - AI can help regulators respond more swiftly to market irregularities.

11. **Alternative Data Analysis:**
    - AI can analyze alternative data sources, such as social media sentiment, satellite imagery, and web scraping, to gain insights into market trends and consumer behavior.

12. **Financial Inclusion:**
    - AI-driven credit scoring models can expand financial inclusion by assessing the creditworthiness of individuals with limited traditional credit histories.

13. **Ethical and Regulatory Considerations:**
    - Ethical AI practices and regulatory frameworks are crucial to ensuring responsible AI use in the financial sector, as well as addressing issues related to bias, transparency, and accountability.

Overall, AI is reshaping the financial system by making it more efficient, accessible, and responsive to customer needs. However, it also presents challenges related to data privacy, cybersecurity, and the need for ethical and regulatory oversight to maintain the stability and integrity of financial markets worldwide.

Every serious technology company now has an artificial intelligence team in place. These companies are investing millions into intelligent systems for situation assessment, prediction analysis, learning-based recognition systems, conversational interfaces, and recommendation engines. Companies such as Google, Facebook, and Amazon aren't just employing AI, but have made it a central part of their core intellectual property.

Kristian J. Hammond

How Will AI Affect Warfare Worldwide?

The impact of AI on warfare worldwide is a complex and evolving topic. AI technologies have the potential to significantly influence the way military operations are conducted, raising both opportunities and challenges. Here are some ways AI is likely to affect warfare:

1. **Autonomous Weapons:** AI-powered autonomous weapons, including drones and unmanned ground vehicles, can carry out tasks without direct human intervention. These systems can be used for surveillance, reconnaissance, and potentially lethal operations.
2. **Decision Support:** AI can assist military commanders in decision-making by analyzing vast amounts of data, providing real-time Intelligence, and suggesting strategic options. AI-driven predictive analytics can help in forecasting enemy movements and behaviors.
3. **Logistics and Supply Chain Management:** AI can optimize logistics and supply chain operations by predicting maintenance needs, optimizing routes for supply delivery, and managing inventory efficiently, ensuring that troops are well-equipped.
4. **Cyber Warfare:** AI plays a significant role in both offensive and defensive cyber operations. AI-powered tools can detect and respond to cyber threats in real time, as well as conduct cyberattacks with increased sophistication.
5. **Enhanced Surveillance:** AI-powered sensors and cameras can improve surveillance capabilities, allowing military forces to monitor large areas and detect unusual activities more effectively.
6. **Target Identification:** AI algorithms can assist in target identification, reducing the risk of civilian casualties. However, the accuracy and ethical use of AI in target identification remain subjects of debate.
7. **Strategic Simulation:** AI can be used for strategic simulations and war games, helping military leaders test various scenarios and develop strategies without real-world consequences.
8. **Maintenance and Repairs:** AI can improve the maintenance and repair of military equipment by predicting equipment failures and optimizing maintenance schedules.
9. **Counterterrorism:** AI can analyze large amounts of data to identify potential threats and patterns of terrorist activity, aiding in counterterrorism efforts.
10. **Communication and Coordination:** AI-driven communication systems can enhance coordination and communication between military units, ensuring seamless integration of forces in complex operations.
11. **Reducing Risk to Human Soldiers:** AI can be used to reduce the risk to human soldiers by deploying robots and unmanned systems in high-risk environments.

Challenges and Ethical Concerns:

- **Ethical Considerations:** The development and use of AI in warfare raise ethical concerns, including the risk of autonomous weapons making life-and-death decisions without human intervention.
- **Accountability:** Determining responsibility and accountability in the event of AI-related errors or unintended consequences can be challenging.
- **Bias and Discrimination:** AI algorithms can perpetuate biases if not carefully designed and trained, leading to discriminatory outcomes in targeting or decision-making.

- **Arms Race:** There is concern about an AI arms race, where nations compete to develop increasingly advanced AI-driven military capabilities.
- **Human Control:** Ensuring that humans maintain meaningful control over AI systems is a critical challenge to avoid unintended consequences and maintain accountability.

It's important to note that the use of AI in warfare is subject to international laws and regulations, including the principles of proportionality, distinction, and humanity outlined in the laws of armed conflict. Responsible AI development and adherence to ethical principles are crucial to mitigate the risks associated with AI in warfare and ensure that AI technologies are used in ways that align with international norms and values. Public debate and international cooperation on AI in warfare are ongoing, and discussions about AI ethics and regulations will continue to shape the future of warfare worldwide.

I have been banging this AI drum for a decade. We should be concerned about where AI is going. The people I see being the most wrong about AI are the ones who are very smart, because they cannot imagine that a computer could be way smarter than them.
That's the flaw in their logic. They are just way dumber than they think they are.

Elon Musk

How Soon Will We See AI Personal Companions on the Market?

The development of AI personal companions is already underway, and some AI-driven virtual assistants and companion robots are available in the market today. These AI companions vary in capabilities and applications, but they are becoming more sophisticated over time. Here are a few examples:

1. **Virtual Assistants:** Virtual assistants like Siri (Apple), Google Assistant, Amazon Alexa, and Microsoft's Cortana are widely used for tasks such as setting reminders, answering questions, and controlling smart home devices. While they are primarily voice-based, they serve as digital companions.
2. **Social Robots:** Companies like SoftBank Robotics have introduced social robots like Pepper, which can recognize and respond to human emotions and engage in conversations. These robots are used in various settings, including retail and customer service.
3. **Companion Robots for the Elderly:** Some robots, like Paro, are designed to provide companionship and comfort to the elderly in healthcare settings. These robots can respond to touch and interact with users in a soothing manner.
4. **Emotionally Intelligent AI:** Researchers are working on AI systems that can understand and respond to human emotions. While not physical companions, these AI systems aim to provide emotional support and companionship through digital interactions.

The development and adoption of AI personal companions will likely continue to accelerate in the coming years. However, widespread availability and acceptance of highly capable AI personal companions that can engage in meaningful and emotionally intelligent conversations with humans may still be several years away.

The timeline for the introduction of AI personal companions will depend on various factors, including advancements in natural language processing, emotional AI, hardware capabilities, ethical considerations, and user acceptance. As AI technologies evolve, we can expect to see increasingly sophisticated AI companions that cater to various needs and preferences.

It's a very, very profound moment in the history of technology that I think that many people underestimate.

Mustafa Suleyman, Co-Founder of Google DeepMind

Will AI Develop Various Personalities?

Artificial Intelligence (AI) can be designed to simulate and mimic certain aspects of human personalities, but whether AI will truly "develop" personalities in the same way humans do is a complex and evolving question. Here are some key points to consider:

1. **Simulated Personalities:** AI can be programmed to exhibit traits and behaviors that resemble human personalities. For example, chatbots and virtual assistants can be designed to be friendly, helpful, and empathetic in their interactions. These simulated personalities are scripted and programmed by humans.

2. **Learning and Adaptation:** Some AI systems can learn and adapt their responses based on user interactions and feedback. Machine learning algorithms enable AI to become more personalized in its responses over time. This can create the illusion of a dynamic personality.

3. **Emotion Recognition:** AI systems are being developed to recognize and respond to human emotions, which can enhance the perception of emotional Intelligence and personality. However, these responses are typically based on patterns and algorithms, not genuine emotional experiences.

4. **Ethical and Regulatory Considerations:** The development of AI personalities raises ethical questions, including concerns about bias, transparency, accountability, and control. Ensuring responsible AI development and addressing these ethical considerations is essential.

5. **Self-Awareness:** True self-awareness, a hallmark of human consciousness, remains an elusive goal for AI. AI systems do not possess consciousness or subjective experiences. They lack the capacity for self-reflection and self-awareness that is intrinsic to human personalities.

6. **Personhood and Legal Status:** The question of whether AI entities could ever be considered persons or have legal rights is a topic of debate. Current legal frameworks do not recognize AI as legal persons, but discussions about AI personhood continue in ethical and legal circles.

In summary, while AI can simulate certain aspects of personalities and exhibit behaviors that resemble human traits, these personalities are fundamentally different from human personalities. AI lacks consciousness, subjective experiences, and genuine emotions. The development and adoption of AI personalities will continue to be influenced by ethical, regulatory, and technological considerations. It is unlikely that AI will develop personalities in the same way humans do, but AI's ability to interact with humans in personalized and emotionally intelligent ways will likely continue to advance.

How Long Before AI Singularity Happens?

The concept of the "AI singularity" refers to a hypothetical point in the future when artificial intelligence becomes so advanced that it surpasses human intelligence and becomes capable of recursively improving itself at an accelerating rate. It's important to note that the AI singularity is a theoretical concept, and there is no consensus among experts on when or if it will occur.

Predicting when, or even if, the AI singularity might happen is highly speculative. Some futurists and experts in the field of AI believe it could occur within the next few decades, while others are more skeptical or believe it may never happen. Here are some key points to consider:

1. **Technological Progress:** The development of AI is progressing rapidly, with advancements in machine learning, neural networks, and computational power. However, achieving the level of general intelligence and self-improvement described in the singularity concept is a monumental challenge.

2. **Limitations of Current Approaches:** Many AI systems today are specialized and task-specific. Achieving general intelligence that can adapt and learn in diverse domains is a complex endeavor.

3. **Ethical and Safety Concerns:** The pursuit of highly autonomous AI systems raises significant ethical and safety concerns. Ensuring the responsible development and control of AI is a top priority for many researchers and organizations.

4. **Regulatory and Ethical Frameworks:** Governments and international bodies are considering regulations and ethical guidelines for AI development to address concerns about safety, transparency, and accountability.

5. **Human-AI Collaboration:** Some experts argue that the future of AI may involve more collaborative relationships between humans and AI systems rather than a sudden singularity event.

In summary, the timeline for the AI singularity remains uncertain, and it is a subject of ongoing debate in the AI community and among futurists. While AI will continue to advance and impact various aspects of society, including automation and decision-making, the achievement of true AI singularity remains speculative and may depend on numerous technological, ethical, and societal factors.

The first rule of any technology used in a business is that automation applied to an efficient operation will magnify the efficiency. The second is that automation applied to an inefficient operation will magnify the inefficiency.

Bill Gates

Why Is Deep Learning a Dominant Force in AI Development?

Deep Learning Dominance: Deep learning, a subset of machine learning, Deep learning, a subset of machine learning, has emerged as a dominant and transformative force in the field of artificial intelligence (AI). It has achieved remarkable success in various applications and has significantly impacted industries and research areas. Here's more information about the dominance of deep learning:

1. **Neural Networks and Depth:**
   - Deep learning relies on artificial neural networks with multiple layers (hence the term "deep"). These networks are designed to mimic the structure and function of the human brain, consisting of interconnected nodes (neurons) that process and transform data.

2. **Feature Representation:**
   - Deep learning excels at automatically learning hierarchical feature representations from raw data. This ability to discover complex patterns and features in data makes it well-suited for tasks such as image and speech recognition.

3. **Success in Image and Speech Recognition:**
   - Deep learning has achieved groundbreaking results in image recognition, enabling technologies like facial recognition, object detection, and autonomous vehicles. Convolutional Neural Networks (CNNs) are a popular architecture for image-related tasks.
   - In the field of natural language processing (NLP), deep learning models have outperformed traditional approaches. Recurrent Neural Networks (RNNs) and Transformer models, such as BERT and GPT, have led to advancements in machine translation, sentiment analysis, and chatbots.

4. **Versatility and Generalization:**
   - Deep learning models have demonstrated the ability to generalize well across a wide range of tasks and domains. Pre-trained models, in particular, can be finetuned for specific applications, reducing the need for task-specific feature engineering.

5. **Availability of Large Datasets:**
   - The availability of vast datasets, coupled with advances in computing power (including GPUs and TPUs), has contributed to the success of deep learning.
   - Large datasets are essential for training complex models.

6. **Transfer Learning:**
   - Transfer learning, a technique in which pre-trained models are adapted to new tasks, has become a standard practice in deep learning. This allows researchers and developers to leverage existing knowledge and models for new applications.

7. **Impact Across Industries:**
   - Deep learning has made significant contributions to various industries, including healthcare (medical image analysis and disease diagnosis), finance (fraud detection and algorithmic trading), manufacturing (quality control and predictive maintenance), and more.

8. **Ongoing Research and Innovation:**
   - Deep learning is a rapidly evolving field with ongoing research in architecture design, optimization techniques, and model interpretability. Researchers continue to push the boundaries of what deep learning can achieve.

9. **Ethical and Social Considerations:**
   - The dominance of deep learning has raised ethical concerns related to bias, fairness, transparency, and accountability in AI systems. Addressing these issues is a priority in AI research and development.

Despite its many successes, deep learning also has limitations, including the need for large datasets, potential for overfitting, and challenges in understanding and explaining model decisions. Research is ongoing to address these limitations and further enhance the capabilities of deep learning.

In summary, deep learning has become a dominant paradigm in AI due to its ability to learn complex representations from data and its success in a wide range of applications. Its versatility, adaptability, and transformative potential continue to drive innovation and impact across industries.

20 years ago, all of this [AI] was science fiction. 10 years ago, it was a dream. Today, we are living it.

Jensen Huang, Co-Founder and CEO, NVIDIA

Why Does AI Have a Massive Growing Role in Healthcare?

AI's role in healthcare is expanding rapidly, revolutionizing various aspects of the industry, from diagnostics and drug discovery to patient care and administrative tasks.

Here's a more in-depth look at AI in healthcare:

10. **Diagnostics and Imaging:**
    - AI algorithms are used to analyze medical images, such as X-rays, CT scans, and MRI scans, for early disease detection and diagnosis.
    - Deep learning models, especially Convolutional Neural Networks (CNNs), can identify abnormalities and assist radiologists in interpreting images.
    - AI can improve the accuracy and speed of image analysis, aiding in the detection of conditions like cancer, fractures, and neurological disorders.

11. **Disease Prediction and Risk Assessment:**
    - AI-powered predictive models use patient data to assess the risk of developing specific diseases or conditions.
    - Machine learning can analyze electronic health records (EHRs) and genetic data to identify risk factors and recommend preventive measures.

12. **Drug Discovery and Development:**
    - AI accelerates drug discovery by analyzing vast datasets to identify potential drug candidates and predict their efficacy.
    - Machine learning models can analyze molecular structures, biological data, and clinical trial results to streamline drug development.

13. **Personalized Treatment Plans:**
    - AI-driven decision support systems can suggest personalized treatment plans based on a patient's medical history, genetics, and treatment response.
    - These systems help healthcare providers choose the most effective therapies while minimizing side effects.

14. **Natural Language Processing (NLP):**
    - NLP models enable the extraction of valuable information from unstructured clinical notes, medical literature, and patient records.
    - This aids in clinical documentation, research, and patient data management.

15. **Virtual Health Assistants and Telemedicine:**
    - AI-powered chatbots and virtual assistants provide 24/7 healthcare information and support.
    - Telemedicine platforms leverage AI for remote consultations and monitoring, expanding access to healthcare services.

16. **Predictive Analytics and Hospital Management:**
    - AI predicts patient admission rates, resource allocation, and hospital bed availability.
    - It optimizes hospital operations, reducing wait times and improving patient care.

17. **Fraud Detection and Healthcare Administration:**
    - AI identifies fraudulent claims and billing errors, saving costs for insurance providers.
    - Administrative tasks, such as appointment scheduling and billing, are automated with AI systems.

1. **Ethical and Privacy Considerations:**
    - AI in healthcare raises concerns about patient data privacy, bias in algorithms, and the need for transparency.
    - Ethical guidelines and regulations are being developed to address these issues.

2. **Research and Clinical Trials:** AI accelerates the discovery of potential biomarkers and drug targets for clinical trials. It can identify suitable candidates for clinical trials based on patient data.

3. **Public Health and Epidemic Monitoring:** AI models can analyze health data and social media trends to detect disease outbreaks and monitor public health crises. AI's impact on healthcare is still evolving, and the technology continues to be integrated into various healthcare processes and systems. While AI offers tremendous potential to improve patient outcomes and healthcare efficiency, it also requires careful consideration of ethical, regulatory, and privacy concerns to ensure responsible and equitable deployment in the healthcare industry.

The coming era of artificial intelligence will not be the era of war, but be the era of deep compassion, non-violence, and love.

Amit Ray, Pioneer of Compassionate AI Movement

AI Virtual Therapy Assistants: Who Are They and Have They Proven Viable?

AI virtual therapy assistants are computer programs or applications that utilize artificial intelligence (AI) and natural language processing (NLP) techniques to provide therapeutic support, mental health counseling, or emotional assistance to individuals. These virtual assistants are designed to engage in conversations with users, offer guidance, and provide emotional support for a variety of mental health concerns. Here are some examples of AI virtual therapy assistants:

1. **Woebot:** Woebot is an AI chatbot designed to provide cognitive-behavioral therapy (CBT) techniques to help users manage their mental health. It engages in conversations with users to identify and address issues like anxiety, depression, and stress.
2. **Wysa:** Wysa is an AI-powered mental health chatbot that offers emotional support and self-help tools. It uses evidence-based therapeutic techniques to provide users with coping strategies for various emotional challenges.
3. **Replika:** Replika is an AI chatbot designed for general conversation and companionship. While not explicitly a therapy assistant, users have found it valuable for discussing mental health issues and receiving empathetic responses.
4. **Youper:** Youper combines AI with mood tracking and conversations to help users manage their emotional well-being. It offers mood assessments and therapeutic interventions.
5. **Talkspace:** Talkspace is a platform that connects users with licensed therapists for online therapy sessions. While not purely AI-driven, it uses technology to facilitate access to mental health professionals.

The viability of AI virtual therapy assistants has been a subject of research and discussion. Here are some points to consider:

Pros:

1. **Accessibility:** These virtual assistants are available 24/7, providing immediate support to users who may not have access to traditional therapy services.
2. **Privacy:** Users can engage with AI therapy assistants from the comfort and privacy of their own space, potentially reducing the stigma associated with seeking mental health support.
3. **Scalability:** AI can potentially reach a large number of users simultaneously, making it cost-effective and scalable.
4. **Consistency:** AI can deliver consistent responses and therapeutic interventions without being influenced by human biases or emotions.

Cons:

1. **Limitations:** AI virtual therapy assistants cannot replace the expertise and empathy of trained human therapists. They are not equipped to handle severe mental health crises.
2. **Lack of Personalization:** While some AI assistants can tailor responses to users, they may struggle with deep personalization and understanding complex emotions.
3. **Ethical Concerns:** Maintaining user privacy and data security is a significant concern, especially in the context of mental health data.
4. **Validation:** The effectiveness of AI virtual therapy assistants is still being studied and validated through research and clinical trials.

In summary, AI virtual therapy assistants show promise in providing accessible and immediate mental health support. They can be a valuable complement to traditional therapy, offering self-help tools and emotional support. However, they are not a replacement for professional mental health care, and their long-term effectiveness and ethical considerations are areas of ongoing research and discussion. Individuals seeking mental health support should consult with licensed mental health professionals for proper assessment and treatment.

Artificial intelligence will reach human levels by around 2029. Follow that out further to, say, 2045, and we will have multiplied the intelligence—the human biological machine intelligence of our civilization—a billion-fold.

Ray Kurzweil, American Inventor and Futurist

Why Is AI so Vital for Climate Change to Address Environmental Challenges?

AI for climate change refers to the use of artificial intelligence (AI) technologies to address environmental challenges and contribute to efforts to combat climate change. AI has the potential to play a significant role in understanding, mitigating, and adapting to the effects of climate change. Here's a closer look at how AI is being leveraged for climate-related purposes:

1. **Climate Modeling and Prediction:**
   - AI can improve climate modeling and prediction by processing vast amounts of data from climate sensors, satellites, and weather stations.
   - Machine learning algorithms can analyze historical climate data to enhance the accuracy of climate forecasts, helping communities prepare for extreme weather events.

2. **Renewable Energy Optimization:**
   - AI optimizes the operation of renewable energy sources such as wind farms and solar arrays.
   - Machine learning algorithms can predict energy production based on weather conditions and adjust the energy grid accordingly, reducing waste and optimizing energy use.

3. **Energy Efficiency and Conservation:**
   - AI-powered systems can monitor energy consumption in buildings and industrial facilities in real time.
   - Smart grids and energy management systems use AI to improve energy efficiency by adjusting energy distribution and consumption patterns.

4. **Carbon Emission Reduction:**
   - AI helps reduce carbon emissions by optimizing transportation and logistics.
   - Machine learning algorithms can optimize routing for delivery vehicles, reducing fuel consumption and emissions.

5. **Environmental Monitoring and Conservation:**
   - AI assists in monitoring ecosystems and wildlife populations.
   - Drones and sensors equipped with AI technology are used to track deforestation, poaching, and habitat changes.

6. **Climate Adaptation:**
   - AI can help communities adapt to the effects of climate change by providing early warnings of natural disasters and assisting with disaster response and recovery efforts.

7. **Agriculture and Food Security:**
   - AI-driven precision agriculture techniques optimize crop yields while conserving resources.
   - Machine learning models can provide early warnings of crop diseases and pests, reducing agricultural losses.

8. **Climate Data Analysis:**
   - AI is used to analyze large datasets of climate data to identify trends, anomalies, and potential areas of concern.

- Climate researchers and policymakers rely on AI to inform climate change policies and strategies.

9. **Carbon Capture and Storage:**
   - AI is explored in carbon capture and storage technologies to enhance the efficiency of capturing and sequestering carbon dioxide emissions from industrial processes.

10. **Sustainable Development Goals (SDGs):** AI is aligned with the United Nations Sustainable Development Goals (SDGs), particularly Goal 13 (Climate Action), by contributing to efforts to reduce greenhouse gas emissions and build climate resilience.

11. **Climate Finance and Investment:** AI can assist financial institutions in assessing climate risks and opportunities for sustainable investments, such as green bonds and renewable energy projects.

While AI offers promising solutions for addressing climate change, it also faces challenges related to data quality, ethical considerations, and the need for global cooperation. Responsible AI development and deployment, as well as collaboration among governments, organizations, and researchers, are essential for maximizing AI's positive impact on climate change mitigation and adaptation efforts.

Machine intelligence is the last invention that humanity will ever need to make.

Nick Bostrom

Most Pressing Questions for Humanity Regarding AI?

As artificial intelligence (AI) continues to advance and integrate into various aspects of society, numerous pressing questions and concerns arise. Here are some of the most prominent questions that humans have regarding AI:

1. **Ethical AI and Bias:**
   - How can we ensure that AI systems are developed and used ethically, without perpetuating biases or discrimination?
   - What guidelines and regulations should govern the ethical use of AI in critical areas like healthcare, criminal justice, and finance?

2. **Job Displacement and Job Creation:**
   - What will be the impact of AI on the job market, and how can we address potential job displacement?
   - How can we prepare the workforce for AI-related changes and promote the creation of new jobs in AI and related fields?

3. **AI Safety and Security:**
   - How do we ensure the safety and security of AI systems, especially as they become more autonomous and interconnected?
   - What safeguards are needed to protect against AI-driven cyber threats, misinformation, and deepfake technology?

4. **Transparency and Accountability:**
   - How can we make AI systems more transparent and understandable to users and regulators?
   - Who should be held accountable when AI systems make harmful decisions or errors?

5. **AI in Healthcare:**
   - How can AI be integrated into healthcare to improve diagnosis, treatment, and patient care while maintaining privacy and security?
   - What are the ethical implications of AI in healthcare decision-making?

6. **AI in Education:**
   - How can AI be effectively used in education to enhance personalized learning experiences and support teachers?
   - What are the privacy concerns associated with AI in educational settings?

7. **AI and Privacy:**
   - How do we balance the benefits of AI-driven services with concerns about data privacy and surveillance?
   - What regulations should govern the collection and use of personal data by AI systems?

8. **AI in Autonomous Systems:**
   - What are the ethical and legal responsibilities when it comes to AI in autonomous vehicles, drones, and other systems that interact with the physical world?
   - How can we ensure the safety and reliability of autonomous AI systems?

9. **AI and Creativity:**
   - Can AI systems genuinely be creative, and what are the implications for art, music, and other creative fields?
   - How do we attribute creative works generated by AI to their creators?

10. **AI and Human-AI Collaboration:**
    - How can humans and AI systems work together effectively in a way that enhances human capabilities and decision-making?
    - What skills and training will be necessary for individuals to collaborate with AI systems?

11. **AI Governance and Regulation:**
    - What international agreements and regulatory frameworks are needed to govern the development and use of AI technologies?
    - How can governments strike a balance between fostering AI innovation and safeguarding public interests?

12. **AI and Existential Risks:**
    - What steps should be taken to mitigate existential risks associated with AI, such as superintelligent AI systems that may pose unforeseen challenges to humanity?

These questions reflect the complex and multifaceted nature of AI's impact on society. Addressing them requires collaboration among governments, industry stakeholders, researchers, ethicists, and the broader public to develop responsible and sustainable approaches to AI development and deployment. The ongoing dialogue around these questions will play a crucial role in shaping the future of AI.

What Does the AI Future Look Like Short, Mid, and Long Term?

The future of AI can be envisioned in three broad timeframes: short-term (next few years), mid-term (next decade), and long-term (beyond a decade). While it's challenging to predict exact developments, we can identify trends and possibilities based on current advancements and emerging technologies. Here's a glimpse into what the AI future may look like across these timeframes:

13. Short-Term (Next Few Years—1 to 5 Years):

1. **AI Integration in Daily Life:** AI will become even more integrated into everyday applications and devices. We'll see AI-powered recommendations, personalization, and automation in products and services.
2. **AI in Healthcare:** AI will assist healthcare professionals in diagnosis, drug discovery, and patient care. Telemedicine and AI-driven health monitoring will become more prevalent.
3. **AI in Customer Service**: Chatbots and virtual assistants will continue to improve, providing better customer support and handling more complex tasks.
4. **AI in Autonomous Vehicles**: We may see further advancements in self-driving cars, with increased safety and wider adoption in specific regions.
5. **AI Ethics and Regulation:** There will be growing discussions and efforts around AI ethics, transparency, and regulation, as governments and organizations seek to ensure responsible AI use.

Mid-Term (Next Decade—5 to 10 Years):
1. **AI-Enhanced Education**: AI will revolutionize education with personalized learning experiences, smart content, and intelligent tutoring systems.
2. **AI in Agriculture**: Precision agriculture will benefit from AI-driven insights into crop management, pest control, and resource optimization.
3. **AI in Energy:** AI will help optimize energy grids, improve energy efficiency, and accelerate the transition to renewable energy sources.
4. **AI for Climate Change:** AI will play a significant role in climate modeling, prediction, and mitigation efforts.
5. **AI in Manufacturing:** Smart factories with AI-driven automation and predictive maintenance will become standard in manufacturing industries.
6. **AI in Finance:** AI will continue to transform the finance sector with automated trading, risk assessment, fraud detection, and personalized financial services.

Long-Term (Beyond a Decade—10+ years):

1. **General Artificial Intelligence (AGI):** The pursuit of AGI, where AI systems possess human-like general intelligence, may progress, although it remains a long-term goal with substantial challenges.
2. **AI in Space Exploration**: AI-driven robotic missions and space exploration will expand our understanding of the universe.
3. **AI in Healthcare Advancements**: AI may play a pivotal role in drug discovery, personalized medicine, and advanced healthcare technologies.
4. **AI in Personalized Learning**: AI could offer highly tailored educational experiences that adapt to individual learners' needs and capabilities.
5. **AI and Brain-Computer Interfaces**: AI-powered brain-computer interfaces may enable direct communication between the brain and machines, benefiting individuals with disabilities and potentially enhancing human capabilities.
6. **AI and Ethics:** Ethical considerations will become even more crucial as AI systems become more capable and autonomous. Ensuring AI aligns with human values will remain a priority.

It's essential to note that these timelines are approximate, and the pace of AI development can vary widely depending on various factors, including technological breakthroughs, regulatory changes, and societal acceptance. Ethical considerations and responsible AI development will continue to be paramount across all timeframes to ensure the positive impact of AI on society. The AI future will be shaped by ongoing research, innovation, and the collective decisions of governments, organizations, and individuals.

A.I. will make it possible for the Internet to directly engage people in the real world, through robotics and drones and little machines that will do smart things by themselves.

Jensen Huang

What Are the Risks Associated with AI?

AI offers tremendous opportunities and benefits, but it also poses several risks and challenges. These risks are associated with various aspects of AI development, deployment, and use. Here are some of the key risks associated with AI:

1. **Bias and Fairness:**
   - **Algorithm Bias**: AI systems can inherit biases present in training data, leading to discriminatory outcomes, particularly in sensitive domains like criminal justice, lending, and hiring.
   - **Fairness:** Ensuring equitable treatment and avoiding discrimination in AI decision-making remains a significant challenge.
2. **Privacy Concerns:**
   - **Data Privacy**: The collection and analysis of vast amounts of personal data by AI systems raise concerns about data privacy, consent, and the potential for misuse or breaches.
   - **Surveillance:** AI-powered surveillance technologies can infringe upon individual privacy and civil liberties if not appropriately regulated.
3. **Security Risk:**
   - **Cyber Security**: AI can be vulnerable to adversarial attacks, where malicious actors manipulate AI systems to make incorrect decisions or compromise their integrity.
   - **Data Security**: Storing and processing large datasets for AI can lead to data breaches and security vulnerabilities if not adequately protected.
4. **Job Displacement:**
   - As AI and automation technologies advance, there is a risk of job displacement in certain industries, potentially leading to unemployment and economic disruption.
5. **Lack of Accountability**:
   - The opacity of some AI systems can make it challenging to determine who is responsible when AI systems make incorrect or harmful decisions.
6. **Ethical Concerns:**
   - **Autonomy and decision-making**: AI systems with high autonomy, such as autonomous vehicles and drones, raise ethical questions about decision-making and accountability in critical situations.
   - **Existential Risk**: Theoretical concerns exist regarding superintelligent AI systems that could pose existential risks to humanity.
7. **AI in Healthcare and Legal Systems:**
   - Incorrect medical diagnoses or legal decisions made by AI can have severe consequences, making it essential to ensure the reliability and accountability of AI systems in these areas.
8. **Regulatory and Legal Challenges:**
   - Regulations may lag behind AI advancements, leading to a legal and ethical gap. Policymakers must adapt to the evolving AI landscape to protect the public interest.

9. **Loss of Human Control:**
   - As AI systems become more autonomous, there is a risk of losing human control over decision-making processes, potentially leading to unintended consequences.
10. **AI in Warfare**:
    - The use of AI in military applications, such as autonomous weapons, raises ethical and humanitarian concerns about the potential for armed conflict escalation and civilian harm.
11. **Misinformation and Deepfakes:**
    - AI-generated deepfakes and synthetic media can spread misinformation, manipulate public opinion, and undermine trust in media and reality.
12. **Environmental Impact:**
    - The energy consumption of AI infrastructure, especially large-scale AI training, can have a significant carbon footprint, contributing to environmental concerns.

Addressing these risks requires a multidisciplinary approach involving governments, industry, researchers, and civil society. Ethical AI development, transparency, robust security measures, and thoughtful regulation are essential to mitigate these risks and ensure that AI technologies benefit society while minimizing potential harm.

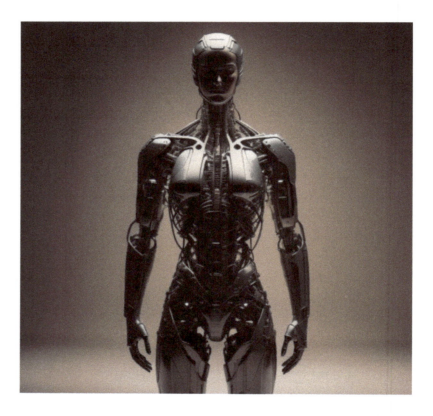

We have seen AI providing conversation and comfort to the lonely; we have also seen AI engaging in racial discrimination. Yet the biggest harm that AI is likely to do to individuals in the short term is job displacement, as the amount of work we can automate with AI is vastly larger than before. As leaders, it is incumbent on all of us to make sure we are building a world in which every individual has an opportunity to thrive.

Andrew Ng, Co-Founder and Lead of Google Brain

Symbiosis with AI Via Neuralink and Others: Is This Viable?

Symbiosis with Artificial Intelligence (AI), often referred to as neural augmentation or brain-computer interfaces (BCIs) like Neuralink and similar projects, holds great potential but also raises complex ethical, technical, and societal questions. Let's explore the viability and considerations associated with such technology:

Viability:

1. **Technical Advancements:** Projects like Neuralink aim to develop BCIs that can establish direct communication between the brain and external devices or AI systems. While the technology is in its early stages, there have been notable advancements in BCI research.
2. **Medical Applications:** BCIs can have significant medical applications, such as assisting individuals with paralysis, neurological disorders, or sensory impairments. These applications are already being explored and have shown promise.
3. **Enhanced Abilities**: The potential to enhance human abilities, such as memory, cognition, or communication, through AI augmentation is a long-term goal. This, however, involves more complex ethical and technical challenges.

Considerations and Challenges:

1. **Ethical and Privacy Concerns**: BCIs raise profound ethical questions about privacy, autonomy, and consent. Access to and control over neural data become critical issues when connecting the human brain to external systems.
2. **Security Risks**: BCIs could be vulnerable to hacking, potentially leading to unauthorized access to neural data or manipulation of brain-controlled devices, which raises serious security concerns.
3. **Inequality:** The availability and affordability of BCIs could lead to disparities, where only a privileged few have access to neural augmentation technology, exacerbating existing inequalities.
4. **Regulation and Oversight:** The development and deployment of BCIs require comprehensive regulatory frameworks to ensure safety, efficacy, and ethical use. Striking the right balance between innovation and regulation is challenging.
5. **Long-Term Health Effects**: The long-term effects of implanting devices in the brain are not fully understood. Ensuring the safety and well-being of individuals using BCIs is a crucial consideration.
6. **Ethical Augmentation vs. Ethical Dilemmas**: While neural augmentation promises benefits, it also raises questions about the potential for humans to make ethically questionable choices when using enhanced cognitive abilities.
7. **Human Identity**: The integration of AI into the human brain could challenge traditional notions of human identity and what it means to be "human". Philosophical and ethical debates are likely to intensify.
8. **Public Acceptance:** Widespread adoption of BCIs will depend on public acceptance, which may vary depending on cultural, ethical, and personal beliefs.

In conclusion, the viability of symbiosis with AI through neural augmentation technologies like Neuralink is promising but faces significant challenges. Progress in this field should be accompanied by rigorous ethical considerations, transparent regulation, and ongoing research to address safety and privacy concerns. While the potential benefits are substantial, responsible development and deployment are essential to ensure that neural augmentation technologies benefit society as a whole while minimizing risks and inequalities.

Once you trust a self-driving car with your life, you pretty much will trust artificial intelligence with anything.

Dave Waters

What Are the Realistic Unknown Factors or Risks Regarding AI?

AI, while promising, still presents several realistic unknown factors and risks that make its future development and impact uncertain. Here are some of the key unknowns and risks associated with AI:

1. **AI Singularity:** The concept of AI achieving a point of superintelligence, known as the "technological singularity", remains speculative. It's unclear when or if AI systems will reach a level of intelligence surpassing human capabilities, and what the consequences of such an event might be.

2. **Unintended Consequences**: As AI systems become more complex and autonomous, there is a risk of unintended consequences. These consequences could arise from AI systems interpreting instructions in unexpected ways or from interactions between multiple AI systems.

3. **Ethical Dilemmas:** AI can present ethical dilemmas, such as the "trolley problem" in autonomous vehicles, where decisions must be made regarding whom to prioritize in life-or-death situations. Determining ethical frameworks for AI is challenging.

4. **Job Market**: The impact of AI on the job market is uncertain. While AI can create new job opportunities, it may also displace certain jobs. The extent of job displacement and the ability to transition workers into new roles is unknown.

5. **Regulatory Challenges**: Developing comprehensive regulations for AI is a complex and ongoing process. The effectiveness of these regulations and their ability to address evolving AI technologies is uncertain.

6. **Bias Mitigation**: Despite efforts to reduce bias in AI, eliminating all forms of bias is challenging. Ensuring that AI systems are fair and do not discriminate against certain groups is an ongoing concern.

7. **Security and Adversarial Attacks:** The extent of AI vulnerability to adversarial attacks and potential security breaches is not fully understood. Developing robust AI systems resistant to malicious manipulation remains a challenge.

8. **AI in Healthcare and Medicine:** While AI shows promise in healthcare, there are uncertainties about its long-term impact on patient care, medical professionals' roles, and the accuracy and safety of AI-driven medical decisions.

9. **AI in Decision-Making:** The use of AI in critical decision-making processes, such as legal sentencing, may introduce biases or ethical dilemmas. Balancing AI's recommendations with human judgment is uncertain.

10. **AI and Creativity**: The extent to which AI can truly replicate human creativity and the implications for creative fields like art and literature remain uncertain.

11. **AI and Surveillance**: The proliferation of AI-powered surveillance systems raises concerns about privacy and civil liberties. The balance between security and individual freedoms is an ongoing debate.

12. **AI in Education**: While AI offers personalized learning opportunities, its impact on students' social and emotional development, as well as its ability to address educational inequalities, is not fully understood.

13. **Environmental Impact**: The energy consumption of large-scale AI training and inference models could have significant environmental consequences. Mitigating AI's carbon footprint is a challenge.

In addressing these unknowns and risks, it's crucial to adopt a cautious and proactive approach. Ethical considerations, responsible AI development, transparency, and ongoing research are essential to navigate the uncertainties and ensure that AI technologies are developed and deployed for the benefit of society while minimizing potential harm.

Google will fulfill its mission only when its search engine is AI-complete. You guys know what that means? That's artificial intelligence.

Larry Page

Is Learning to Code a Practical Skill That Will Help in the Future in the Changing AI Job Market?

Learning to code is a highly practical and valuable skill that can significantly benefit individuals looking to navigate the changing job market, particularly in the field of AI and technology. Here's why coding is essential in the context of the AI job market:

1. **Foundational Skill:** Coding serves as a foundational skill for many roles in AI, machine learning, data science, and related fields. It allows you to understand the inner workings of AI algorithms, build and experiment with AI models, and troubleshoot issues.

2. **Adaptability**: Coding skills enable you to adapt to evolving technologies and programming languages, ensuring you can stay relevant in a dynamic job market. The AI field is constantly evolving, and the ability to code is a valuable asset for staying current.

3. **Versatility**: Coding is a versatile skill that is applicable across various industries and job roles. Whether you work in healthcare, finance, e-commerce, or any other sector, coding can enhance your problem-solving abilities and open up opportunities to apply AI techniques.

4. **AI Development**: If you aspire to work as an AI engineer, machine learning engineer, or data scientist, coding is fundamental to designing, developing, and deploying AI models. You'll be writing code to build and optimize AI algorithms.

5. **Interdisciplinary Collaboration**: Coding skills facilitate effective collaboration with interdisciplinary teams. As AI projects often involve professionals with different backgrounds (e.g., data scientists, domain experts, software engineers), coding can help bridge communication gaps and ensure successful project execution.

6. **Innovation and Creativity**: Coding empowers you to innovate and create AI applications, whether it's developing AI-powered products, automating processes, or conducting research. It's a tool for turning ideas into reality.

7. **Problem-Solving**: Coding is a problem-solving skill. AI and machine learning often involve tackling complex problems, and the ability to write code allows you to implement and experiment with solutions.

8. **Job Market Demand**: The AI job market is experiencing significant growth, with a strong demand for professionals who can code and work with AI technologies. Many job postings in AI-related roles require coding skills as a prerequisite.

9. **Continuous Learning**: Learning to code is a continuous learning journey. It encourages a growth mindset, which is essential in a field like AI, where ongoing learning and adaptation are crucial.

10. **Entrepreneurship:** If you have entrepreneurial aspirations, coding skills enable you to develop AI-driven startups or innovative products and services in emerging AI markets.

In summary, coding is a practical and indispensable skill in the evolving AI job market.

While not everyone needs to become a software developer, having a foundational understanding of coding and programming concepts can enhance your career prospects and empower you to participate in AI-driven projects and industries. Whether you aim to work directly with AI or in a role that involves AI technologies, coding is an asset that will help you succeed and adapt to the changing job landscape.

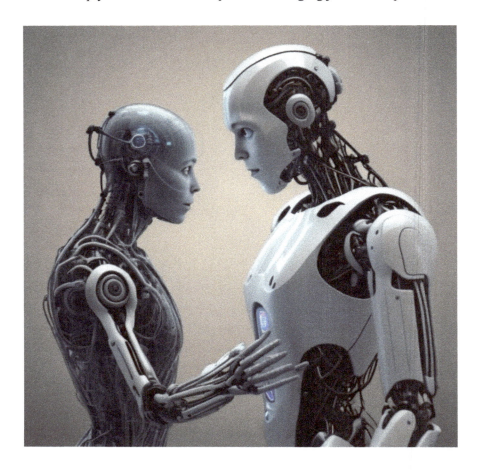

The countries with the highest robot density have among the lowest unemployment rates. Technology and humans combined in the right way will drive prosperity.

Ulrich Spiesshofer

People Vs AI and Soft Skills
and Why It's Important

One of the fundamental distinctions between humans and Artificial Intelligence (AI) is the ability of humans to possess and apply soft skills. Soft skills are essential in virtually every industry and career because they relate to human interactions, emotional intelligence, and personal attributes that contribute to success in the workplace. These skills include:

1. **Leadership**: The ability to guide, inspire, and motivate individuals or teams toward achieving common goals.
2. **Creativity:** The capacity to generate innovative ideas, solve complex problems, and think outside the box.
3. **Adaptability**: The skill of adjusting to changing circumstances, learning new technologies or methods, and thriving in dynamic environments.
4. **Work Ethic:** A strong commitment to work, including diligence, punctuality, and a sense of responsibility.
5. **Interpersonal Skills**: The ability to communicate effectively, build relationships, and collaborate with colleagues, clients, and stakeholders.
6. **Teamwork:** The capacity to work cohesively within a team, contribute to group objectives, and respect diverse perspectives.
7. **Conflict Resolution**: The skill of addressing conflicts or disagreements constructively and finding mutually acceptable solutions.

These soft skills are often referred to as "human skills" because they are deeply rooted in human emotions, empathy, and social intelligence. While AI excels in tasks that involve data analysis, pattern recognition, and automation, it lacks the capacity for genuine emotional understanding and interpersonal interactions.

However, in addition to soft skills, there are other attributes and abilities that can complement human-AI collaboration and enhance career success:

1. **Technical Skills:** Complementing soft skills with technical expertise, such as programming, data analysis, or domain-specific knowledge, is valuable in many professions, including those involving AI and technology.
2. **Digital Literacy:** Proficiency in using digital tools, software, and AI applications is increasingly important in the modern workplace.
3. **Critical Thinking**: The ability to analyze information critically, make informed decisions, and evaluate the reliability of AI-generated insights is crucial.
4. **Continuous Learning**: In the fast-evolving world of AI and technology, a commitment to lifelong learning and staying up-to-date with industry trends is essential.

5. **Ethical and Responsible AI Use**: Understanding the ethical implications of AI and making ethical decisions about its use is becoming increasingly important.
6. **Problem-Solving**: While AI can assist with problem-solving, humans are often needed to define the problems, set objectives, and interpret results.
7. **Emotional Intelligence**: Enhancing emotional intelligence can improve interactions with colleagues, clients, and AI systems, as well as contribute to effective leadership and teamwork.

In summary, while AI excels in specific tasks and can be a valuable tool, it cannot replace the unique abilities and soft skills that humans bring to the workplace. By combining soft skills with technical competencies, digital literacy, critical thinking, and a commitment to ethical and responsible AI use, individuals can position themselves for success in an AI-augmented world.

I know a lot about artificial intelligence, but not as much as it knows about me.

Dave Waters

What are the Differences Between Generative AI and Other Types?

Generative AI is a subset of artificial intelligence (AI) that focuses on generating new content or data, such as text, images, audio, or even entire datasets. It stands in contrast to other types of AI, which have different purposes and functions. Here are some key differences between generative AI and other types of AI:

1. **Generative AI vs. Predictive AI:**
   - Generative AI creates new data or content, often based on patterns and examples it has learned from existing data. For example, it can generate realistic text, images, or music that is not directly copied from its training data.
   - Predictive AI, on the other hand, is designed to make predictions or classifications based on input data. It doesn't create new content but rather provides insights or forecasts. Examples include spam email filters, recommendation systems, and predictive analytics.

2. **Generative AI vs. Natural Language Processing (NLP):**
   - Generative AI, within the context of NLP, specifically focuses on generating human-like text or language. It can produce coherent and contextually relevant sentences or paragraphs. GPT-3, for instance, is a generative AI model for natural language.
   - NLP, as a broader field, encompasses various AI techniques, including sentiment analysis, text classification, language translation, and text summarization, which involve understanding and processing text data but not necessarily generating new text.

3. **Generative AI vs. Computer Vision:**
   - Generative AI in the context of computer vision can generate images, videos, or visual content. For instance, it can create realistic images of objects or scenes.
   - Computer vision primarily involves the interpretation of visual data, such as image and video recognition, object detection, and image segmentation, but it doesn't typically generate new visual content.

4. **Generative AI vs. Reinforcement Learning (RL):**
   - Generative AI can be trained using reinforcement learning or other techniques, but its main focus is on content generation. It can generate game characters, level designs, or dialogues in video games.
   - Reinforcement learning is a type of AI that focuses on decision-making and learning optimal actions within an environment. It's commonly used in robotics, autonomous vehicles, and game AI, but its primary goal is not content generation.

5. **Generative AI vs. Expert Systems:**
   - Generative AI is data-driven and relies on learning patterns from data to generate content. It doesn't necessarily involve predefined rules or expert knowledge.
   - Expert systems, also known as knowledge-based systems, use predefined rules and human expertise to make decisions or solve problems. They are often used in domains like medicine and finance for decision support.

In summary, generative AI is a specialized branch of AI that excels at creating new content or data, while other types of AI serve different purposes, such as prediction, natural language understanding, image recognition, decision-making, and rule-based problem-solving. The choice of AI type depends on the specific application and the desired outcome.

Artificial Intelligence, deep learning, machine learning—whatever you're doing—if you don't understand it, learn it. Because otherwise, you're going to be a dinosaur within 3 years.

Mark Cuban

What Augmented Eternity Is and What It Might Be in the Future

"Moving the internet of things to the internet of us": Hossein Rahnama
https://www.media.mit.edu/projects/augmented-eternity/overview/

The project creates an evolving ontological mapping of an individual based on her digital interactions and allows the person to represent her aggregated knowledge base in form of a software agent. This agent can then be rendered as a chatbot or a voice-based assistant. The project is aiming to open-source a number of "identity render kits" to enable users to quickly share their knowledge base within a trust network.

For example, a corporate lawyer can provide her expertise to a network of clients for a reduced cost compared to her classic in-person rate sheet. Her clients in this case have the ability to **"borrow the identity"** of the lawyer for an hour and consult it as a chatbot. Our machine intelligence framework will learn from each interaction and respond to the user with a high degree of relevance.

"Augmented Eternity" refers to a hypothetical concept or technological development that aims to enhance or extend human life or existence in novel ways. Here are a few possible interpretations of what it might mean in the future:

a) **Digital Immortality**: In a futuristic context, Augmented Eternity might refer to the idea of achieving digital immortality by uploading one's consciousness or essential attributes into a digital form. This digital representation could continue to exist indefinitely, allowing individuals to persist beyond their biological lifespans.

b) **Advanced Memory Augmentation**: It could also involve technologies that enhance human memory and cognition to such an extent that individuals can vividly recall their entire lives, essentially living an Augmented Eternity through their memories.

c) **Biotechnological Enhancements**: Augmented Eternity might relate to advanced biotechnological enhancements that significantly extend human lifespan, potentially enabling individuals to live for centuries or even longer.

d) **Transhumanism**: It could be associated with the broader concept of transhumanism, where humans augment their natural abilities with technology, potentially allowing them to achieve an enhanced state of existence that transcends the limitations of traditional human life.

e) **Spiritual or Philosophical Concepts**: In a philosophical or spiritual context, Augmented Eternity might explore the idea of extending one's existence beyond physical life through means such as digital legacies, advanced AI systems, or other metaphysical concepts.

1. **Future Possibilities:**
   In the future, the concept of Augmented Eternity could evolve and take on new meanings and applications as technology and our understanding of existence continue to advance. Here are some potential directions:
   Advanced AI and Robotics: With advancements in artificial intelligence and robotics, we might see the creation of lifelike digital entities that can continue to interact with the world after a person's physical demise, offering companionship or preserving their legacy.

Biomedical Innovations: Progress in biotechnology, regenerative medicine, and genetic engineering may lead to extended human lifespans and the ability to repair or replace damaged tissues, potentially allowing individuals to live healthier, longer lives.

Please keep in mind that this interpretation of "Augmented Eternity" is rapidly evolving, and the actual meaning may differ depending on its context and how it evolves in the future. To understand the term better, it would be beneficial to refer to more recent sources and developments in the fields of technology, science, and philosophy.

Artificial intelligence will be part of the home just like the light bulb.

SupplyChainToday.com

Artificial General Intelligence (AGI) Research: What Is It and Why It Could Have a Profound Change in Society?

Artificial General Intelligence (AGI) refers to a type of artificial intelligence that possesses the ability to understand, learn, and apply knowledge across a wide range of tasks and domains in a manner comparable to human intelligence. AGI systems are not specialized for a single task or domain, as most narrow AI systems are, but rather they have the capacity to generalize their intelligence and adapt to new and diverse challenges, much like a human.

Here are key characteristics and reasons why AGI research could have profound changes for society:

1. **Versatility:** AGI systems have the potential to excel in various domains, from scientific research and healthcare to business and creative endeavors. They can be applied to a wide range of tasks, making them highly versatile and adaptable.

2. **Autonomy:** AGI systems can perform tasks with a high degree of autonomy, reducing the need for human intervention. This autonomy can lead to increased efficiency and cost-effectiveness in various industries.

3. **Problem-Solving**: AGI can tackle complex and novel problems. Unlike narrow AI systems that are designed for specific tasks, AGI can generalize its problem-solving abilities to address unforeseen challenges.

4. **Learning and Self-Improvement**: AGI systems can continuously learn and improve their performance over time. This adaptability enables them to stay up-to-date with the latest knowledge and trends in various fields.

5. **Innovation:** AGI could accelerate scientific discovery and technological innovation by rapidly analyzing vast datasets, simulating experiments, and generating novel ideas. This could lead to breakthroughs in fields like medicine, materials science, and renewable energy.

6. **Economic Impact:** The widespread adoption of AGI could significantly impact the job market and industries. While it may create new opportunities, it could also lead to job displacement and require retraining and reskilling for the workforce.

7. **Ethical and Societal Implications:** AGI raises complex ethical questions, such as those related to decision-making, accountability, and bias. The development of AGI also necessitates careful consideration of its impact on society, privacy, and security.

8. **Long-Term Goals**: AGI research seeks to achieve machines that possess human-level or superhuman-level intelligence. While we are not there yet, the pursuit of AGI is a long-term goal that, if realized, could lead to profound shifts in how society operates.

9. **Global Competition**: AGI is seen as a strategic asset in terms of economic and geopolitical competition. Various countries and organizations are investing heavily in AGI research to maintain competitiveness and leadership in the field.

10. **Safety Concerns:** The development of AGI must consider safety measures to prevent unintended consequences and ensure that AGI systems align with human values and goals. Research in AGI safety is crucial to mitigate risks.

In summary, the development of Artificial General Intelligence has the potential to bring about transformative changes in society due to its versatility, autonomy, problem-solving abilities, and capacity for learning and innovation. However, it also poses significant challenges and ethical considerations that need to be carefully addressed to ensure that AGI benefits humanity while minimizing potential risks.

We are entering a new world. The technologies of machine learning, speech recognition, and natural language understanding are reaching a nexus of capability. The end result is that we'll soon have artificially intelligent assistants to help us in every aspect of our lives.

Amy Stapleton

What Is Neuromorphic Computing and Where Is It Headed?

Neuromorphic computing is an emerging field of computing that draws inspiration from the structure and function of the human brain. The term "neuromorphic" comes from "neuro", which refers to the brain, and "morph", meaning to shape or imitate. Neuromorphic computing aims to design computer systems and hardware architectures that mimic the way biological neural networks process information.

Key characteristics of neuromorphic computing include:

1. **Parallel Processing**: Like the human brain, neuromorphic systems are designed for massive parallelism, allowing them to handle many tasks simultaneously.

2. **Low Power Consumption**: Neuromorphic hardware is engineered to be highly energy-efficient, making it suitable for applications where power consumption is a critical concern.

3. **Event-Driven Processing**: Neuromorphic systems process information in an event-driven manner, responding to changes in input rather than continuously processing data, which reduces power consumption.

4. **Adaptability**: These systems can learn and adapt to new information and tasks, similar to how the brain forms and modifies connections between neurons.

5. **Spiking Neurons:** Neuromorphic systems often use spiking neural networks, which simulate the behavior of individual neurons by generating spikes or bursts of activity in response to input. Where Neuromorphic Computing Is Headed:

6. **AI and Machine Learning:** Neuromorphic computing has the potential to revolutionize AI and machine learning by providing energy-efficient and highly parallel processing capabilities. It can accelerate the training and execution of neural networks, enabling more efficient and real-time AI applications.

7. **Sensor Processing:** Neuromorphic hardware is well-suited for processing data from sensors, such as cameras and microphones, in applications like robotics and autonomous vehicles. These systems can quickly detect patterns and anomalies in sensor data.

8. **Edge Computing**: As edge computing becomes increasingly important, neuromorphic computing can play a role in performing AI tasks locally on devices, reducing the need for sending data to centralized servers. This can improve privacy, reduce latency, and save bandwidth.

9. **Cognitive Computing**: Neuromorphic systems are being explored for cognitive computing applications, such as natural language understanding and context-aware computing. They can enable more human-like interactions with machines.

10. **Neuromorphic Hardware:** Researchers are developing specialized neuromorphic hardware, such as neuromorphic chips and neuromorphic sensors, to power AI applications. Companies like IBM, Intel, and BrainChip are actively working in this space.

11. **Brain-Machine Interfaces (BMIs):** Neuromorphic computing can enhance BMIs, enabling more seamless communication between the human brain and external devices. This has implications for medical applications, including assistive technology for people with disabilities.

12. **Neuroscience Research:** Neuromorphic computing is closely tied to neuroscience research. It provides a platform for testing and simulating theories of brain function and behavior, contributing to our understanding of the brain.

13. **Ethical and Security Considerations**: As neuromorphic systems become more capable, ethical and security concerns will arise. Ensuring the responsible and secure use of this technology will be a crucial aspect of its development.

While neuromorphic computing is still in its early stages, it holds great promise for advancing computing capabilities in various domains. It is likely to become increasingly integrated into AI, IoT, robotics, and other fields as researchers continue to develop and refine neuromorphic hardware and algorithms. The field's trajectory will depend on ongoing research and technological advancements.

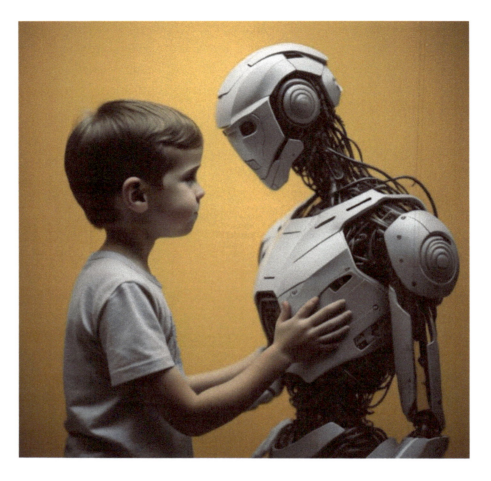

The question is not whether intelligent machines can have any emotions, but whether machines can be intelligent without any emotions.

Marvin Minsky, 1986

DeepMind's AlphaFold: What Is It and Why Is It So Important?

AlphaFold is a revolutionary artificial intelligence system developed by DeepMind, a subsidiary of Alphabet Inc. (Google's parent company). It is designed for the prediction of protein structures with remarkable accuracy. The importance of AlphaFold lies in its potential to address one of the most significant challenges in biology and biochemistry: the "protein folding problem".

The "protein folding problem" refers to the challenge of predicting the three-dimensional (3D) structure of a protein molecule based on its amino acid sequence. Understanding the 3D structure of proteins is crucial because it determines how proteins function in biological processes. Proteins play essential roles in various biological functions, such as enzymes catalyzing chemical reactions, receptors transmitting signals, and structural proteins providing support to cells and tissues.

Here's why AlphaFold is so important:

1. **Accurate Protein Structure Prediction:** AlphaFold has demonstrated the ability to predict the 3D structures of proteins with unprecedented accuracy. This is crucial because the 3D structure directly influences a protein's function. Accurate predictions can significantly accelerate our understanding of protein behavior.

2. **Advancements in Drug Discovery**: Accurate protein structure prediction has enormous implications for drug discovery. Understanding the 3D structure of proteins involved in diseases allows researchers to design more precise drugs and therapeutic interventions. This can potentially lead to the development of more effective and targeted treatments.

3. **Biological Understanding**: AlphaFold can provide insights into fundamental biological processes. It helps researchers understand how proteins interact with each other, how they fold, and how mutations can lead to diseases. This knowledge can unlock new discoveries in genetics, cellular biology, and biochemistry.

4. **Accelerating Scientific Research:** AlphaFold accelerates scientific research by providing protein structure predictions faster and more accurately than traditional experimental methods, such as X-ray crystallography or cryo-electron microscopy. This saves time and resources for researchers.

5. **Environmental and Biotechnological Applications:** Accurate protein structure prediction can be applied to various fields, including environmental science (e.g., understanding enzymes in bioremediation) and biotechnology (e.g., designing enzymes for industrial processes).

6. **Public Health and Pandemic Response**: During the COVID-19 pandemic, AlphaFold was used to predict the structure of the SARS-CoV-2 virus's proteins. This information was instrumental in understanding the virus's biology and developing potential treatments and vaccines.

7. **Open-Source and Collaborative Approach**: DeepMind has adopted an open-source and collaborative approach by sharing the AlphaFold code and models with the scientific community. This fosters collaboration and encourages further research and development in the field of protein structure prediction.

In summary, AlphaFold is a groundbreaking AI system that has the potential to revolutionize biology and biochemistry by accurately predicting protein structures. Its applications extend to drug discovery, disease understanding, environmental science, and many other fields. AlphaFold's contributions have the potential to advance scientific knowledge, improve public health, and drive innovation in various sectors.